Love Answering Love

Praying through the Bible

— NEIL G. RICHARDSON —

Sacristy
Press

Sacristy Press
PO Box 612, Durham, DH1 9HT

www.sacristy.co.uk

First published in 2023 by Sacristy Press, Durham

Sacristy Limited, registered in England & Wales, number 7565667

British Library Cataloguing-in-Publication Data
A catalogue record for the book is available from the British Library

ISBN 978-1-78959-279-5

Contents

Why praying today might be a problem

Lord . . . why do you hide your face from me?

Psalm 88:14

Then Jesus told them a parable about their need to pray always and not to lose heart.

Luke 18:1

A lifelong churchgoer informed his minister that he had given up on prayer; "it didn't work". That may be true for many people today. We feel we're not getting anywhere. Or a prayer hasn't been answered. Or we've grown out of earlier ways of praying and not found alternatives. Or—most often perhaps these days—we find it hard to make time to pray.

Prayer, like belief in God, is too important to give up on. An old hymn describes prayer as "the Christian's vital breath". Unfortunately, prayer rarely seems as simple and natural as breathing. Our breathing, of course, can be improved, as the instruction "take deeper breaths" implies. But is prayer simply a matter of "practice makes perfect"? According to the Bible, it's not quite like that, even though the Bible encourages us to persevere in prayer.

In the Christian tradition, prayer and reading the Bible go together. We can pray without reading the Bible, and we can read the Bible whether we pray or not. But each should enrich the other. Our prayers can be shallow and often self-centred when we don't learn from the Bible, and Bible reading without prayer easily becomes academic and arid.

Christians tend to think of prayer as talking to God. But is that what prayer really is? Prayer certainly includes telling God what is on our hearts. But the Bible and later Christian tradition suggest that it's more than that. The Bible offers no "quick fixes" for our prayers, no shortcuts to success (whatever that may be). But it will show us what prayer is—and, in the process, invite us to discover life itself.

Life is easily taken for granted if we're not struggling each day to survive. But that's part of our problem. Taking life for granted slides into taking our Creator, God, for granted. And that's not all. Sometimes we run away from life: we hide from things, pretend to ourselves, run away from other people—or some of them!

Our way of life today doesn't make praying easy. The modern world has brought enormous benefits to a fast-growing number of people. But there are new pressures on the human spirit as well. Silence and wisdom, in particular, seem to be in short supply, and it remains an open question whether the human race in the twenty-first century will flourish or self-destruct. Now is not the time to neglect either prayer or the Bible.

So how can praying and reading the Bible enrich each other? That is the concern of this book.

Praying and believing—Which comes first?

Do we need to believe in order to pray—or, at least, pray well? Many of us will know or know of people who pray without believing—at least in the traditional Christian sense. People in a crisis often find themselves praying, whatever they have previously believed or not believed about God.

Christian belief today has been sharply challenged. In the so-called developed world, believers are growing fewer. Or, at least, most churches are less well attended than they were. Many people assume that the Christian religion is old hat. (Or is it possible it's widely misunderstood—even in churches?) Scandals in the Church don't help. The writings of atheists such as Richard Dawkins appear to threaten long-held beliefs.

Yet believing is vital in the practice of prayer. Believing and praying stand or fall together. It's not easy to sustain one without the other. They go together—like praying and reading the Bible. But, as we shall see, praying as the Bible portrays it includes a lot of questions and doubts about God—and protests and anger galore.

What does "believing" involve? It is more than believing *that* God exists. It is believing *in* God—the beginnings of trusting God and committing ourselves to God, however tentatively at first. That kind of believing, for Christians, grows out of the revelation of God in Jesus of Nazareth. Believing in God and in Jesus go closely together.

But we can't make ourselves believe. So how do we get started?

George McLeod, the founder of the Iona Community in Scotland, was once asked how he would help a person who wanted to believe in God. He replied, "I would tell him to 'make-believe' in Him—act always as if God were alive. He would, by experience, come to know God."[1]

Now that may sound like playing imaginary games rather than engaging with reality. And it could be. Yet, as I believe the Bible shows, prayer is a journey towards reality: towards discovering our real selves and the real God—as opposed to substitutes and counterfeits for both. On that journey we begin to discover life as it's really meant to be lived and the world as it really is—contrary to our lopsided, distorted views of both. That journey takes time. The journey towards belief is the same.

George McLeod's suggestion means living *as if* God is real—even on days when we're not sure, and can never have proof—*and living accordingly.* Marriage at its best is an illustration. Proof doesn't come into it—or, rather, the proof is to be found in the living and in the relationship, out of which an initial trust and commitment grow deeper still.

On not taking God for granted

Many people today practise "mindfulness" or other forms of meditation. Valuable as these can be, they are not the same as prayer. The Bible doesn't offer advice or techniques for getting in touch with our inner selves or for dealing with stress. But, as I hope this book will show, the Bible can lead us to our truest, deepest selves and, in the process, help us live more resiliently amongst all the pressures of contemporary life.

---

[1] Ronald Ferguson, *George McLeod, Founder of the Iona Community* (London: W. Collins, Sons & Co Ltd., 1990), pp. 80–1.

Prayer in the Bible involves an engagement, even a conversation, with God. Our journey towards the reality which is God may begin before we believe very much at all in the traditional sense. But even if I only *begin* to believe, that tentative beginning may still be the time to say some simple basic prayers. At this early stage, we can begin to ask: to whom or to what are we praying?

One of the most attractive arguments for Christian faith in recent years has been Francis Spufford's *Unapologetic: Why, Despite Everything, Christianity Can Still Make Surprising Emotional Sense*. That may seem a daunting title. Yet behind the title is a warm, personal story.

After a ghastly day and night dominated by blazing rows at home, Francis Spufford was sitting in abject misery in a café drinking cappuccino. Whilst he was there, the café proprietor played a cassette: the slow movement of Mozart's Clarinet Concerto. That music, Spufford wrote, "sounded the way mercy would sound". That's an unusual word, easily misunderstood. What he meant was: the universe isn't as random as many suppose, but is "sustained by a continual and infinitely patient act of love" and "that love keeps it in being".[2] Despite what we think, the universe—or rather, the power behind, above, beneath the universe—is warmer and kinder than we realize.

The experience led Spufford to believe, not in a God who "micro-manages" the universe, but in a God "who is continually present everywhere anyway, undemonstratively underlying all cafes, all cassettes, all composers; when God is the ground of our being . . .".[3] The word "undemonstratively" is important. God doesn't impose himself on us. God is anything but the domineering cosmic bully which Richard Dawkins and others have made God out to be. "A still small voice" is easily ignored. In contrast to the many strident counterfeit gods, the real God is more reticent, courteous and less obvious—as God is likely to be if, as the Bible claims, God is Love (1 John 4:8,16).

---

2   Francis Spufford, *Unapologetic: Why, Despite Everything, Christianity Can Still Make Surprising Emotional Sense* (London: Faber & Faber Ltd., 2012), p. 20.

3   Spufford, *Unapologetic*, p. 73.

Francis Spufford's experience in the café illustrates what the Bible claims. We are never outside God's presence; rather, God is the One who is always near, whatever it may feel like—as close and all-embracing as the air we breathe. People of deep faith and prayer have always said as much.

So while God is far from obvious, God's presence everywhere—even though hidden—means that, as the Bible tells us, his Spirit breathes through creation. (The Hebrew and Greek words for "spirit" in the Bible also mean "breath" or "wind".) Yet the personal nature of God, revealed—as Christians believe—especially in Jesus, means that God isn't just a spiritual environment. God can be experienced as a companion and friend.

For many of us, childhood images of God may linger on—like God "answering" prayers as if he were a celestial being operating a huge telephone exchange. One of the problems for many of us, whether Christian or not, is leaving behind inadequate images of God. In place of them, we need what I would call a strong doctrine of providence. That grand old word doesn't mean God has pre-ordained everything that happens, or even that God knows in advance what will happen. It is more in keeping with the Bible's teaching to think of God as the One who *provides* what we really need when we pray. That is what the Spirit seeks to do in human minds and hearts, drawing or nudging us towards truth, wisdom and grace. It is a "Providence" outside of which we cannot fall.

Living as if God is real has practical consequences. For example, we shall be less inclined to take life for granted but, instead, live it thankfully. "The surest way to suppress our ability to understand the meaning of God ... is to take things for granted."[4] It also commits us to living as generously as we can towards others simply because, if God is real, by definition God is the Creator of everyone. And if this Creator is, as Christian faith claims, a God who *is* love, then loving others becomes a major outcome of the practice of prayer—even if all we can manage to start with is "God, are you real?"

---

[4]   Christopher Bamford, "Washing the Feet", in Lorraine Kisly (ed.), *The Inner Journey: Views from the Christian Tradition* (Sandpoint, ID: Morning Light Press, 2006), p. 173.

There is no such thing as private prayer

Where do other people fit in? And, more specifically, where does the Church fit in? Why can't I just pray at home and do my own thing? My family told me once, on my return from an early Sunday service, that the small number of people who attended were those who wanted to avoid everyone else! That may not have been an entirely serious remark, but making a habit of avoiding other people is hardly Christian living.

It's easy to tell horror stories about churches. Many people no longer go to church because of bad experiences: "the vicar refused to marry us", "no one spoke to us" . . . the charge sheet is a long one. Church services can be boring, unintelligible and unrelated to life and the wider world. But in the Christian tradition going to church and praying belong together. I don't mean, of course, that only churchgoers pray. That is clearly not so. Yet prayer divorced from the prayers and worship of the Church is likely to become a more spasmodic, private and even idiosyncratic affair—little more than a shopping list for God. The Bible, by contrast, portrays a kind of praying which, though personal, is not a private affair at all. In the Old Testament individuals pray as members of the people of Israel. In the New Testament, the followers of Jesus pray "in Christ" with others.

In spite of its many failures, the Church stands for something fundamental to our wellbeing and the wellbeing of the world. Other people matter, and they matter as much as everyone else, including each of us. The Church teaches us to pray not only with other human beings but also for them. Left to ourselves, we are likely to pray first and foremost for ourselves and for our nearest and dearest. But Christian faith invites us to a much wider and more demanding kind of praying for others. It's an integral part of the Church's vocation.

A welcoming, lively church can be the road back to prayer and to belief in God. There are many good stories to balance the horror stories. As one person remarked to the visitor from church, "Since coming to know you, it seems I'm coming to know God, too." There is nothing anti-social about prayer. Drawing closer to God does not mean distancing ourselves from other people—the life and teaching of Jesus demonstrate the opposite. If we're serious about prayer, we shall be serious also about church, warts and all. Times of solitude, of course, if and when they are possible, are invaluable. But we can't and shouldn't always pray on our own. We need other people. The Bible's perspectives here are crucial—sometimes surprising, often challenging, but never less than encouraging.

So, to revert to this section's title, there is no such thing as private prayer, if by that we mean prayer which is my business, and no one else's—my personal hotline to God. Prayer in private? Yes—Jesus encouraged it (Matthew 6:5–6). Personal prayer? Of course.

Conclusion

Pray as you can: that is the advice of many great teachers of prayer. Pray just as you are, without pretending or wishing you are better than you are. Pray in the place where you have to be without wishing you were somewhere else. If you can find a place conducive to prayer, so much the better. And pray in a way that comes naturally to you.

"Pray as you can." Our prayers don't have to be put into words. God already knows what we want and what we need, and doesn't need to be informed about anything. But, to begin with, we shall probably need to put our prayers into words. Most important, do we mean what we are saying? We may hope we do, but, again, whether we do or not, God knows.

What to pray? Well, start with whatever is on your heart to say— even if your first thought is to wring the neck of someone who has just embarrassed or disappointed you. That has to be worked through, but the golden rule is: honesty before God. Or we can start with the Lord's Prayer, even if we're not sure what it all means. What matters is that our life of prayer develops and grows, even if progress is difficult and even dangerous to measure. If we think we're progressing, we're probably not. If we think we're hopeless at it, that could be a good sign.

On this lifelong, life-enhancing journey, the Bible will be a precious resource. But you may not be at all sure about that.

Prayer

Lord, on good days I think I believe. On bad days, I'm far from sure. On many a day in between, I often waver. Help me to take time to wonder, to be thankful, to live in the present, to put more of myself into what I have to do each day, and, meanwhile, simply to trust.

For reflection and discussion

1. Does praying help us to believe? Does believing help us to pray?
2. Living "as if" God is real: do you already do this, and, if so, what difference do you find it makes?
3. Is the advice "Pray as you can" helpful or not? Or does it let us off the hook?

2

Why reading the Bible today might be a problem

Whatever was written . . . was written for our instruction, so that by steadfastness and by the encouragement of the scriptures we might have hope.

Romans 15:4

So also our beloved brother Paul wrote to you . . . There are some things in them [sc. his letters] hard to understand, which the ignorant and unstable twist to their own destruction, as they do the other scriptures.

2 Peter 3:15–16

Can the Bible help us in our prayers? Many people who would own the name "Christian" have given up on the Bible, or never really got started on any kind of devotional reading of it. Some will be aware of the many criticisms and questions posed about the Bible since the advent of modern biblical scholarship and science. The debate "creation or evolution?" continues. Atheists such as Peter Hitchens and Richard Dawkins have protested about the violence of God in the Bible. Feminist writers have pointed out its often patriarchal character. The list could be extended.

For many people, the Bible—or, at least, large tracts of it—constitutes a problem. Even if we bracket out books which we might consider less important, there are still many passages in the Psalms, the Gospels and the letters (especially of Paul) which are stubbornly difficult. Can the Bible really resource and deepen our prayers?

This chapter gives a brief account of my own journey in working through some of the problems and challenges the Bible presents, shows how easily our reading of the Bible can be skewed by our own misconceptions, and reflects on how we might think of the Bible as both human and divine.

A brief conclusion will outline what the authority of the Bible means in practice.

A personal journey: Can we keep it simple?

I began to read the Bible long before I studied theology and became, eventually, a teacher of the New Testament. There was an innocence about my Bible reading as a young Christian; I can't recall questioning or doubting anything in the Bible in those days! Bible-reading notes helped me through my teenage years and beyond.

In those days, I hardly noticed the differences between the Gospels—still less the contradictions. I read Old Testament stories, too, without wondering whether God really ordered Joshua to massacre the inhabitants of Jericho. Nor did I question what to make of Paul's command to the Corinthians that women should cover their heads in church (1 Corinthians 11:1–16). (My mother wouldn't have dreamed of going to "chapel" without wearing a hat.)

Such was the innocence of my teens. And for me there can be no going back. (Someone, on hearing of Darwin's theory of evolution, prayed "Lord, may it not be true; or at least, if it is, may it be hushed up.") Whatever the failures and limitations of modern biblical scholarship— and they are real enough—we cannot now put the genie back in the bottle. Like modern science, it's here to stay. Like science, biblical scholarship has enormous achievements to its credit. At its best, it is liberating and illuminating. It liberates us from untenable views of the Bible which we are better without. It also sheds light on biblical passages which are obscure or difficult or both. But the new knowledge and ideas it brings can be unsettling and disturbing.

An early crisis of faith for me occurred when a teacher at school lent me Renan's *Life of Jesus*. The opening pages left me wondering whether

Jesus really had risen from the dead. I returned the book to the teacher in some haste, giving an emphatic "No" to his amused question "Didn't you like it?"

My later theological studies raised many questions for me, transforming my understanding of the Bible. They still do. As I look back on the way I have come, I observe a strange paradox. The more I have studied the Bible, the more questions about it and objections to it I have encountered. Yet the authority of the Bible "shines" more than ever for me; the Bible is a companion inseparable from my prayers. The journey has made me realize that simplicity is not something we leave behind, but a spiritual state we travel towards. I shall return to this apparent paradox at the end of this chapter.

An early stage of the journey involved the discovery that the stories of the Bible are not straightforward accounts of what actually happened. We have tended to think that an event narrated in the Bible in the past tense must therefore have happened. But that can't be entirely true, as when there are different versions of the same story.

Even the Gospels fail to score maximum points for historical accuracy. It's often suggested that people who watch the same football match report it differently. But this is an analogy which doesn't fit the Gospels. Even though original eyewitnesses first passed on these stories, the Gospel writers themselves weren't eyewitnesses, and Matthew and Luke almost certainly used an edition of Mark's Gospel in writing theirs. Again, there are often two or three versions of the same parables and miracles of Jesus. Jesus no doubt told a parable more than once, but some of Matthew's and Luke's versions sometimes contain what we might call their distinctive trademarks as writers. That would suggest that they have edited the versions they had come across.[1]

Many Christians think the authority of Scripture is under threat if we can't be sure about, for example, exactly what Jesus said and did—quite

---

[1]   The Beatitudes (Matthew 5:3–12 and Luke 6:20–3) and the Lord's Prayer (Matthew 6:9–15 and Luke 11:2–4) are important examples of different versions of Jesus' teaching. Most scholars do not think the disciple Matthew was the author of the Gospel which bears his name. As with the other Gospels, "according to . . . " was a title added later.

apart from Old Testament stories which raise all sorts of questions. But we don't read the Bible just for historical information. Using our imaginations thoughtfully and prayerfully as we read is more important. Imagine, for example, Jesus washing Judas' feet (John 13:5,21–30), or the disciples recognizing the risen Jesus by his scars (John 20:20); we read the Bible because it contains—*and conveys*—truth which is life-giving, a revelation which has begun to change the world. That's the secret of its authority.

Our understanding of that authority can grow as we get to know the Bible better, and, crucially, face the awkward questions it raises. For the sake of the maturity of our faith, we have to work through these questions. Life in general and the Christian life in particular involve living with questions.

The argument can be taken too far. If the Bible was nothing but fables, the heart would be torn out of both the Jewish and Christian faith. But that has never been demonstrated, and after the dedicated, painstaking scholarship of the last three centuries, it is most unlikely it ever will be. The Church tradition that Scripture "containeth all things necessary for our salvation" still stands.

We don't read the Bible as we would read other books. We savour and "chew" the words—in the presence of God, seeking not just lessons to apply to life, but immersing ourselves in the words, attending to them and trying to hear them. That's a long, slow discipline—but infinitely worthwhile.

A not-so-good reader meets an ugly Bible

That sounds an unpromising mix: a poor reader and a Bible which some find offensive and, in parts, ugly. But let me introduce myself as a poor reader, as my journey continued. I realized that we can go for years without hearing what the Bible *really* says. I had long assumed that Saul of Tarsus became "Paul" when he met Jesus on the Damascus Road (Acts 9:1–20). It was a shock to be told that he didn't; that happened four chapters later (Acts 13:9). The example is not important in itself, but it illustrates how easily we fail to notice the text; we assume it says what we've always thought it says. Or we simply miss the significance of the details. The novelist-friend of C. S. Lewis, Charles Williams, once observed that some people believe the Bible and some people don't; but neither group *notices what the words are.*

Sometimes the problem is not what we mistakenly think the Bible says, but the wrong associations which a key word in the Bible has acquired. The name "Pharisee" is an important example. Somewhere in the past I had learned to think of the scribes and Pharisees as reactionary bigots who couldn't or wouldn't recognize the Son of God when they saw him. I had also read that the Judaism of Jesus' and Paul's day was a legalistic, rule-bound religion, teaching salvation by "works"—i.e. trying to earn our salvation. Now I began to discover that these views were inaccurate caricatures, or worse.

This matters a great deal. Dramatized versions of Gospel stories in church services sometimes trivialize Jesus' encounters with the Pharisees, portraying them as figures of fun. But if we trivialize these encounters, we trivialize both Scripture and the gospel itself. Even if Jesus caricatured a Pharisee in one of his parables (Luke 18:9–14), his audience would have known it, and would have grasped the parable's subversive implications. The Pharisees, like St Paul before his conversion, had "a zeal" for God and God's law (Galatians 1:14; Romans 10:2)—like many Christians today ("If the cap fits . . . ")!

Our frequent caricaturing of the Pharisees illustrates how easily we read into the text ideas and even words—as my example about Paul's name shows—which simply aren't there. It's like not listening properly to, or seriously misunderstanding, what someone is saying to us. There is a fine line between reading out of the text what *is* there, and reading into it what isn't. We can't and shouldn't be detached, objective readers of the Bible but, as in any serious conversation, we have to be attentive, patient listeners.

There is a place for sometimes questioning a literal interpretation of the Bible. At an evening service once, the reader of the epistle startled us by announcing at the end, "This is not the word of the Lord." She smiled as she said it, but we knew why. She had just read the words "Wives, obey your husbands" (Colossians 3:18), one of many verses in the Bible demonstrating the male-dominated world of the time. I have sometimes found it helpful to ask: "If that is what St Paul wrote then in that culture, what would he write now in ours?" It would surely not be the same. Paul also wrote, with reference, probably, to the first five books of what we call the Old Testament " . . . the letter kills, but the Spirit gives life" (2 Corinthians 3:6). It applies equally to the New.

In the 1970s and 1980s, I began to see that other people, including many women, read and interpreted the Bible differently from me. The Bible's male imagery of God was and is a problem for many. Images of God such as "king", "lord" and even "father" can be unhelpful—and misunderstood. The Bible as a whole—and Jesus in particular—turns upside down traditional hierarchies of status and power, including patriarchy. But facing up to this can be a long, hard journey, especially if we have a male image of God.

Christians in countries which used to be European colonies have also had good cause to be critical of the Bible. As Archbishop Desmond Tutu observed, when the British came to Africa, the Africans owned the land. The British taught them to read the Bible and to close their eyes to pray; when they opened their eyes, their land had gone. Similarly and tragically, the influence of the conquest narratives of the Book of Joshua on the white settlers of the USA, Australia and New Zealand was a disaster for many of the original inhabitants of those countries.[2]

I come to one of the later stages of my journey. Divine violence in the Bible—from the stories of the Flood and the destruction of Sodom and Gomorrah (Genesis 19:24–5) onwards—is a problem which Christians have been slow to face. But stories like these must surely be read in the light of the fundamental Christian conviction that God is love. There is divine violence in the New Testament, as well as the Old, especially, but not only, in the book of Revelation. It may come down to a choice between believing that God is wholly love, or keeping our earlier view of the Bible's authority at the expense of God's moral credibility.[3] (Qualifying God's love by, say, God's holiness or justice, as many Christians have done, is to misunderstand both.)

---

[2]   See my *Who on Earth is God?* (London: Bloomsbury, 2014), pp. 54–6.
[3]   *Op. cit.*, Chapter 2, "Moses, Joshua and the Violence of God".

Biblical scholarship, like modern science, is here to stay. It isn't infallible; it develops and changes. But we can't ignore biblical scholarship, or pigeon-hole it as an academic approach to Scripture. A great New Testament scholar used to say that "academic theology" is a contradiction in terms. Similarly, a theologian is, as the Eastern Churches have taught, *one who prays*. So there need be no serious conflict between mind and heart in our praying and in our reading of the Bible. Yet some may wonder, in the light of this spiritual odyssey, what is left of biblical authority. That is the subject of the final section of this chapter.

Is the Bible human and divine?

The Church has traditionally believed that Jesus was fully human and fully divine. Can the same be said of the Bible? I begin with the humanness of the writers of the biblical books.

Some years ago, I was surprised to read, in a commentary on 1 Corinthians by an eminent Catholic scholar, that St Paul's sarcastic jibes at the Corinthians, expressed in 1 Corinthians 4:8, were pastorally unwise. No wonder, the writer suggested, that the apostle got into trouble at Corinth, and had to write more letters!

My point here is not whether that scholar was right, but whether an inspired writer of Scripture could have made a mistake—even committed a sin. I eventually concluded, not without a struggle, that inspiration does not make a biblical writer either infallible or morally perfect. Scripture is still the vehicle of a transforming, divine revelation despite—or because of?—human flaws and failings.

The human quality of the Bible and of its writers comes through time and again. That is part of its glory and its authority. But is the Bible still divine—still the Word of God—in spite of Paul losing patience with the churches at Corinth—and some of his critics (see Galatians 5:12)?

Two polar opposite views of the Bible need to be discarded when we read it as Christians. The first view is this: the Bible is "inerrant" *because* it is God's word: no mistakes, no contradictions, no faults of any kind. Such a view flies in the face of the facts and doesn't do justice to the sheer humanness of the Scriptures.

But to say the Bible is all too human—just like any other book—is also mistaken. There is a parallel here with Jesus himself. In calling Jesus fully human and fully divine, the Church rejected the idea that Jesus was a fusion or a watered-down version of both—superhuman and semi-divine. It also refused to separate or isolate the human and the divine; Jesus was one person—as the Bible is one library of books. Divine and human in the Bible belong together, as they do in the person of Jesus:

> The presence of the divine justifies the description of the Bible as the Word of God, and the presence of the human writers secures that this Word is heard in human accents, even if at times they falter.[4]

There is an important difference between Jesus and the Bible. The Church has always believed Jesus was "without sin" (Hebrews 4:15); there was a perfect unity in him of human and divine. But, as with St Paul, there are times when the human limitations of a biblical writer are all too apparent. When the book of Deuteronomy commands the extermination of Canaanites and other peoples (20:16), we have to say "religious zeal can go badly wrong", and people who write in this vein "are completely wrong about what God wants and commands".[5]

It's tempting to hanker after an abridged or expurgated version of the Bible without these all too human sections. But that would be complicated, perhaps impossible, and certainly unwise. Even the most unpromising parts of the Bible can yield important insights—that is, provided we interpret the Bible in love and for love—what one scholar has called "a hermeneutic of love". ("Hermeneutic" comes from a Greek word meaning "to interpret".) We can aspire to love the Bible, "warts and all" as God's gift to us, and read it in order to love God and our neighbour. We will naturally read some parts of the Bible more often than others: Psalm 23 rather than Psalm 59, John's Gospel rather than the middle chapters of Revelation. But what the early Church under the providence

4   John McIntyre, *The Shape of Christology: Studies in the Doctrine of the Person of Christ* (2nd edn, Edinburgh: T & T Clark, 1998), p. 323.

5   Keith Ward, *Word of God* (London: SPCK, 2010), pp. 39–41.

of God joined together, we should not lightly put asunder. An expurgated Bible easily becomes a distorted one.

Conclusion

A distinguished preacher and theologian testifies that, as she became a more "sophisticated interpreter" of the Bible, at the same time she became a more simple believer. The word "sophisticated" might be unhelpful to some. But this dual development is important. We grow in our understanding and knowledge of the Bible *and* we journey towards simplicity.

What might be a good working definition of the authority of Scripture? I suggest this: it is our primary source of *life, truth and growth*.[6] Those are key Christian words: "life" and "truth" are identified with Jesus (John 14:6), and Christian living is about "growing" in Christ (e.g. Ephesians 3:14–19; 4:11–16). The Bible is a source of life, truth and growth in a wider sense. It witnesses to a universe created by God, and also created "in and for Christ" (Genesis 1 and Colossians 1:15–20). To interpret well and to live by the Bible's teaching enhances human wellbeing and the world's.

In the following chapters we shall explore what the Bible has to say about prayer before returning, in a final chapter, to the question of how our prayers and our reading of the Bible might each enrich the other.

Prayer

Lord, help me to be attentive in reading the Bible, to persevere in honesty and courage with its difficulties, and to want more and more its life-giving truth.

---

[6]   Nicholas Lash, *Voices of Authority* (London: Sheed and Ward, 1976).

For reflection and discussion

1. Individually or in a group, try mapping out stages in your own journey in reading and understanding the Bible.
2. Is biblical scholarship a hindrance or a help in reading the Bible? What have been particular challenges or questions for you?
3. Can the Bible be said to be like Jesus—human and divine?

3

The prayer and the call of God

We love because he first loved us.

1 John 4:19

But the Lord God called to the human (adam), and said to him, "Where are you?"

Genesis 3:9

An imaginary preface to the Bible: A letter from God

Dearly Beloved,

As sons and daughters of Adam and Eve, you may be surprised to hear me addressing you like this. But it's true: before the universe came into being, you were in my heart. I foresaw—I planned your coming. At first, you could hardly hear me at all. You were too busy surviving to notice my footprints here and there, or to hear the whisper of my call—often at unexpected times and in unexpected places. Always, I have held you in my heart; from the beginning I have been calling you to life and to love.

Even now, you call me to mind only fleetingly—especially when you are desperate! You seem to think I am far away. Yet I am closer to you than you realize. There is nowhere you may go where I am not. I am above you and beneath you, before and behind you. There is no moment when I'm not there.

It has not been easy for you or me. You know what heartache children can cause their parents. And children can find their parents exasperating! You sometimes wonder if I'm really there at all. But you need space to flourish, and it's not my nature to impose.

In spite of everything, you are still my "beloved". Never once have I allowed my care for you to lapse, my love for you to wane. Meanwhile, what you call "the Bible" is my story and your story, my Word and your words, your prayers and my prayer . . .

We tend to think of prayer as talking to God. But in the Bible it is God, not we, who speaks first. God makes the first call. We may think of that call as God's own prayer to a hard-of-hearing humankind. We begin where the Bible itself begins—with the prayer and call of God to pray, to love—and, in so doing, really to live.

In the beginning was the prayer (of God)

The imaginary letter from God to humankind with which this chapter begins doesn't mean God is a figment of our imagination. Quite the contrary. As the people of earlier centuries used to say, God is "the most real Reality" there is. Even though the Bible is full of stories, that doesn't mean they are not profoundly true. Not all of them are historical, but they still convey truth about God and about ourselves.

So we begin at "the beginning". We can't imagine that, and shouldn't even try. Science may help us to envisage the first "Big Bang" or whatever there was at the universe's first origins, but why there was anything at all in the first place is more mysterious. The Bible simply says, "In the beginning God . . . " (Genesis 1:1).

It's also idle to speculate why God created the world. Even the Bible doesn't tell us, although its first chapter's repeated refrain suggests that sheer delight came into it somewhere: "God saw that it was good . . . " ("Beautiful" would do just as well as a translation of the Hebrew word for "good".) Christian tradition has been content to say that God made the world out of nothing and out of love—a bit like God writing an open-ended drama or an unfinished symphony.

To emphasize the point about the Bible's stories, Noah and the Flood is just that—a story. It's unfortunate that children's versions of this story gaily tell them that "God killed everyone because they were so bad". Of course, there was and is a problem to fix: the state of the world—as news bulletins every day remind us. But there is another message coming through in this ancient story: "Never again", says God, "will I destroy the world". And just to make sure we get the message, God says it four times (Genesis 8:21 and 9:11)—five times, if we count 9:15 as well. God knows now that, with humankind, he's got a problem; he's in for the long haul—no quick or easy fixes. And that's where God's prayer or call to us begins.

There's a hint of it earlier on. "Where are you?", says the Creator to the first human being, hiding in the shrubbery. We humans may have offered our primitive, superstitious prayers down the millennia, but all the time, had we but known it, God has been looking for us. Something odd is going on: we should like whatever gods there are to bail us out—send the rain, save us on the high seas, from pestilence and plague and so on—but when the real God comes looking for us, we run away! Francis Thompson's poem "The Hound of Heaven" describes our flight well:

> I fled Him down the nights and down the days;
> I fled Him down the arches of the years . . . '

To return to the story of Noah, I suggest that we think of the rainbow and the divine promise which accompanies it ("Never again . . . ") as God's own prayer: God's commitment to his world, and God's search for humankind. The Bible not only begins but also ends with this rainbow:

> I have set my bow in the clouds, and it shall be a sign of the covenant between me and the earth.
>
> *Genesis 9:13*

> . . . there in heaven stood a throne . . . and around the throne is a rainbow . . .
>
> *Revelation 4:2–3*

So the prayer of God runs through the Bible like a golden thread.

Sometimes this prayer or call of God to us comes powerfully to expression, as in Isaiah 65:1–2:

I was ready to be sought out by those who did not ask,
To be found by those who did not seek me.
I said "Here I am, here I am",
To a nation that did not call on my name.
I held out my hands all day long to a rebellious people . . .

St Paul quotes part of this divine plea: God "keeps stretching out his hands to us all" (Romans 10:21). This "pathos" of God—as a great Jewish scholar has called it—comes through strongly also in Psalm 81. The Psalmist imagines Israel hearing the voice of the God whom they had not yet encountered, whilst they were still slaves in Egypt:[1]

I hear a voice I had not known:
"I relieved your shoulder of the burden;
Your hands were freed from the basket.
In distress you called, and I rescued you . . . "

verses 5–7

The prayer of God to his people in this psalm continues:

O Israel, if you would but listen to me!

verse 8

This is the picture the Bible gives us of prayer: God prays or speaks first; we may think of it, in the light of all that follows, as the call of love. So whilst we offer our *cris de coeur* to God (and that's what they often—and understandably—are), there is something more profound going on: our Creator reaching out to us in love and prayer. This love and prayer find expression time and again in God's call.

---

[1]   The book of Exodus in the Old Testament tells the story. Even if much of the story is far from historical, its impact, first, on the people of Israel, and, through them, on the life of the world, has been immeasurable.

The call of Love—the start of it all

In the Bible the words "call" and "create" are closely linked: God's creation of us *is* his call—a call to be the human being God created us to be. God's "call" may take many forms: a call to move on in life, to go deeper, to reach outwards—especially to others. The call may be experienced as a niggling feeling of dissatisfaction or restlessness: "there is more to life—and to my life—than I have so far realized". It may be a nudge towards truth—a greater awareness of life and the world around us and a deeper, wider awareness of other people.

God's call may lie within an experience which is making us more self-aware—more honest with ourselves. That experience may well involve suffering of some kind. But it may also come in the form of a wondering thankfulness for the gift of life and life's many joys. It may come through another person's call for help.

God's call is easily missed, but never far away. Responding to it is a step towards a greater openness to life and to other people. If we go on attending to it, it will lead us into a greater openness to God. However this call is experienced, it is the key to the Bible's understanding of prayer. And always, however the call is experienced, the One who calls is nearer to us than breathing, a Love as intimate as a mother's or a father's. We may distance ourselves from God, but God is always near to us, not a long way off in a far-away heaven.

According to the Bible's first stories, God has made us in God's image, and we live only because God's Spirit has breathed life into us (Genesis 1:26–8 and 2:7). So there is an innate "holiness" in us all. That is what "made in God's image" means: we are made to reflect back to God God's own love for and joy in us. This, in the biblical view, is the root of our restlessness: "our hearts are restless until they find their rest in You" (St Augustine).

This is where our story and our prayers begin. The Bible's first two chapters, with their complementary pictures of God, set the scene. The "You" in whom we live is the transcendent, mysterious power from whom everything comes (Genesis 1), and also a close companion who speaks with us, and to whom we may speak (Genesis 2). So in the Bible God calls people by name. Sometimes God repeats a person's name, underlining the urgency of the call, as in "Moses, Moses" (Exodus 3:4) or "Samuel, Samuel" (1 Samuel 3:10). Sometimes God calls and gives a person their true name: Abram becomes Abraham (Genesis 17:5); Jacob becomes Israel (Genesis 32:28), and that name reveals the person's vocation—as in Isaiah 43:1:

> But now thus says the Lord,
> he who created you, O Jacob,
> he who formed you, O Israel:
> "Do not fear, for I have redeemed you ... "

For some the call begins at birth, or even before—as with the prophet Jeremiah and the apostle Paul (Jeremiah 1:5; Galatians 1:15). The hearing of that call marks the beginning of a voyage of self-discovery. So even if we think of God's calling of people by name in the Bible as a detail in a story, it expresses a profound truth. Our first prayers in response are the beginning of a journey towards becoming the human being God intends us to be.

Given the number of people on this planet, God's habit of calling people by name is remarkable. The word "eternal" is not easy to define. It's been suggested that calling God "eternal" means "God has time". So the "eternal" God is not "fazed" by years and distances or, we might add, by the sheer number of people in the world. Unlike us humans, who struggle sometimes to remember even the names of a few people, the eternal God knows everyone by name.

In the New Testament the call of God begins to reach everyone, and it comes through a particular individual—Jesus of Nazareth. This gives a new focus to prayer. In time, though not before the death and resurrection of Jesus, his disciples will pray "in his name" or "through Jesus Christ our Lord". But some biblical patterns continue in the New Testament as in the Old. For example, God's call often comes to people not expecting it (e.g. Mark 1:16–20), to people who prefer not to respond to it (e.g. Luke 9:56–63), but particularly to people who are especially undeserving (e.g. Mark 2:17).

A contemporary writer on prayer refers to God's call as God's "magnetism": "There is a magnetism in God—a wonderful, mysterious something which draws and attracts and pulls us. Like all magnetic forces, it is hidden and unseen; and so it can go unrecognized."[2] This may help to explain a mysterious saying of Jesus, " . . . many are called, but few are chosen" (Matthew 22:14). "Many" was the Jewish way of saying "all", but "few are chosen" might suggest that God becomes more choosy in a second inspection of people he has called. Does this explain why some people are "religious" and some are not? There is a mystery here. Many factors are at work in people's lives, some drawing us to God, some distracting us. But what the Old Testament hints at, the New Testament confirms: God's call embraces everyone. But for those who respond, there can never be grounds for self-congratulation. On that the Bible is almost fiercely insistent. It is God who makes disciples and Christians; there is a mystery of grace at work in our lives, and it's not just what we choose.

The letters of Paul show that God's call is a universal call. Because of Jesus, Gentiles—foreigners, "outsiders"—as well as Jews, are called to faith, to love and prayer. Qualifying for, or earning that call doesn't come into it (e.g. Romans 9–11). You don't have to be "religious" to pray, and God seems to make a point of calling unlikely people who by prevailing standards are not impressive at all. But Paul recognizes that there is a troubling mystery about why some people appear impervious to the call of God, as his long, involved argument in Romans 9–11 shows. The description of God's magnetism, quoted earlier, continues by recognizing the mystery:

> . . . it can go unrecognized, and be ignored, forgotten or doubted.
> We are not always aware of it, and some people never are; but
> it is there . . . [3]

So being "called" is not for a privileged few, even though those who seem to respond to God appear fewer than those who do not. I recall a conversation with a student who thought that it was our choice which made the crucial difference. But that can leave the way open for those who make the "right" choice to congratulate themselves, and to pass judgement

---

[2]   Alexander Ryrie, *The Prayer of Silence* (Fairacres: SLG Press, 2012), p. 5.

[3]   Ibid.

on those who do not—as a story Jesus told about a religious person and a "sinner" (Pharisee and tax collector) suggests (Luke 18:9–14).

What the Bible calls "grace"—God's undeserved love—is the foundation for everything truly Christian. One of my own teachers put it like this: God's grace is "that power which enables us to do what otherwise we would not be able to do". And that includes loving and praying.

God calls us to be human, rather than "religious", a word difficult to define, and so perhaps a word to avoid as much as we can. In any case, as a member of a Christian religious order once remarked in my hearing, it is more important to be human than religious.

Those who are called *first* are called not only for their own sake, but also *for the sake of others*; the universal Creator loves all "the others" just as much. This is bound to shape our prayers. The gospel of Jesus means that, especially in praying, we become less, not more judgemental towards other people:

> Do not judge, so that God will not judge you.
>
> *Matthew 7:1*

In the light of all this, the Bible offers one, and only one, ultimate test of all our praying: is it leading us to love God and other people?

A call to life

The call of God to humankind to find life and love is sometimes expressed as the call of wisdom. Unfortunately, "wisdom" these days is a word seldom heard. Yet it's far too important to neglect or forget. Wisdom isn't about acquiring knowledge or amassing academic degrees. Wisdom, as valued and sought in many religions down the ages, is different. A wise person is someone who understands and sees what life is all about, who sees what really matters in life, and sets their own life by that.

The Bible speaks of a divine wisdom. It is the wisdom of God which has designed the universe and which calls to us all. If we think of it as the very heart and mind of God, we shan't go far wrong. The call of wisdom is expressed in the Book of Proverbs:

Hear how wisdom calls
And understanding lifts up her voice . . .
It is to you I call,
To all mankind I appeal . . .
Those who love me I love,
And those who search for me will find me.

Proverbs 8:1,4,17

What Proverbs says about wisdom is similar to words about Jesus in some of Paul's letters:

By wisdom the Lord laid the earth's foundations.

Proverbs 3:19

The Lord created me [i.e. wisdom] the first of his work.

Proverbs 8:22

Paul writes of the whole universe being made "through Christ". (Colossians 1:15–20 comprise his fullest expression of this idea.) Jesus, as the wisdom of God, reveals the very heart and mind of God, the divine blueprint for the world.

So here is another way of thinking of God's own prayer—the reaching out of Love to the world. It is God's "wisdom" calling to humankind. The most appealing and attractive example of this call comes in Matthew's Gospel. It's not obvious that the words of Jesus express the call of wisdom, but the similarities with another "wisdom" writing in the Apocrypha show that they do:

Come to me, all you that are weary and are carrying heavy burdens, and I will give you rest . . . For my yoke is easy, and my burden is light.

Matthew 11:28–30; cf. the conclusion
to Ecclesiasticus 51:23–27

These words convey one of the mysterious blessings of prayer: divinely given refreshment and strength—as one of the Old Testament prophets promised:

> Those who wait on the Lord will renew their strength.
>
> *Isaiah 40:31*

Prayer is far more than a "hotline" to God. (Prayer is that, too, as the Bible, particularly the Psalms, shows again and again.) It is, above all, a relationship or conversation with God which begins with God's own call to us. But now we must go on to ask: what are human beings getting into as we hear and respond?

God's call to the human race is a call to partnership, with commitments on both sides: God has committed himself to us, and looks for our commitment to him in return. The biblical word for this partnership is "covenant". The relationship promised in Leviticus is the signature tune of the whole Bible:

> ... I will walk among you and will be your God, and you shall be my people.
>
> *26:12*

The promise echoes down the centuries, across the pages of the Bible—for example, Hebrews 8:10, echoing the prophet Jeremiah. It is there at the very end of the Bible:

> See, the home of God is among mortals. He will dwell with them; they will be his peoples [plural in the original Greek]. And God himself will be with them ...
>
> *Revelation 21:3*

Out of God's universal call, God's friendship and God's promises the prayers of humanity grow. Prayer begins in response to the mysterious You who calls us to life. God's call is the beginning of a journey which stretches into the future. In the Bible it takes individuals—and in the case of Israel, an entire nation—into unexpected, sometimes threatening places. That is because God's call in the Bible often comes in the form of a commission: "I have a job for you."

The commission can be an outcome of prayer and worship—as in the case of Isaiah (Isaiah 6:1–8); it may also lead to prayers—of all kinds. (On this see Chapter 4.) This biblical pattern suggests that living before God alerts us to our responsibilities. It reminds us of responsibilities we already knew, or draws our attention to tasks we'd ignored or have never even seen. We don't always know what we're letting ourselves in for when we begin to pray.

According to the story the Bible tells, life "in all its fulness" (e.g. John 10:10) is the direction of travel when we begin to pray. Yet, though a few people, such as monks and nuns, are called to be members of communities specially devoted to prayer, most people live their life with God and for God in very down-to-earth situations. The Bible illustrates very well how interwoven human and divine are in the life of the world, and the call of God is a call to earth our prayers in daily life, as a twentieth-century diary shows:

> The prayerful life in its quintessence does not consist of devotional exercises at particular times . . . but living for God and living with God. Thinking, working, playing, doing everything with a view to God's purpose . . . that is the essence of prayer.[4]

(Prayer at particular times, of course, can be an invaluable aid towards this goal. This, too, the Bible indicates.)

Conclusion

God calls to every human being on this planet: calls us into conversation, into covenant, into a relationship of love. We are "called"—addressed—in a way we have not been addressed before. We may want to hide or to

---

4   Pennar Davies, *Diary of a Soul*, tr. by Herbert Hughes (Tal-y-bont: Y Lolfa, 2011), pp. 24–5.

pretend, but this is a moment of truth: the call of love. The people of Israel, disciples of Jesus and—ultimately—everyone, are God's "beloved".

More disconcertingly, God commissions us to love and serve our fellow human beings. But always God promises and gives even more than he asks for. This is the foundation of our prayers. So praying isn't really a human-centred activity at all. We make our requests to God, but our praying only really takes off when the Real God—as opposed to the god of our imagination—begins to "lift" our prayers. To change the image, we need the wind of God in our sails.

So in the Bible's varied stories of God calling people we begin to see some of the fundamentals of prayer. We become more aware of the personal Reality at the universe's heart, all around us and deep within us. It is a Presence, always and everywhere, springing surprises, never out of reach or earshot. However strange it may seem to say God "hears" (on this see Chapter 4), that is the reality to which the biblical writers bear witness. Of this mysterious, personal Reality—through everything that life could throw at them—biblical writers affirm again and again the Rock of Ages which enables their prayers: "The Lord reigns."

Prayer

Lord, teach me to be still enough to listen and to wonder. Let me not take life or You for granted. Awaken my heart to respond more fully to the Life and Love which you are calling me to discover and to share.

For reflection and discussion

1. We tend to think of God's "call" as a call to something religious. The Bible suggests something broader and deeper: the call to each of us to be the person we have been created to be. Can this perspective help our praying?
2. Can you identify experiences of God's presence?
3. If in a group, share experiences both of "answered" and "unanswered" prayers.

4

It takes two: A conversation begins

O Lord, you have searched me and known me.

Psalm 139:1

Then Mary said, "Here am I . . . "

Luke 1:38

Prayer in the Bible starts with God, not ourselves. God's call in the Garden of Eden to Adam, "Where are you?" sets the scene for the evolution of humankind: our Creator has been looking for us since the beginning of time. God's call to Abraham confirms it. Of course, we have offered our *cris de coeur* to heaven as far back as relics of human life and settlement go. But, according to the Bible, the story really begins with God's own prayer: the call of Love. God initiates a conversation—a relationship with the human race, inviting us to respond. We haven't sought or expected it, still less deserved or—often—even wanted it, but still it comes.

So what light does the Bible shed on how we go about offering our own prayers in response to God's prayer to us? A prayer of C. S. Lewis can help us get started: "The prayer preceding all prayers is, 'May it be the real I who speaks. May it be the real Thou that I speak to'. We begin with 'the real I.'"[1]

---

[1]   C. S. Lewis, quoted in *Prayers and Meditations: Everyman's Library Pocket Poets*, selected and edited by Peter Washington (Everyman's Library, 1995), p. 37.

Honest to God: Locating the real me

Starting with the real me (whoever that is) turns upside down most of our ideas about prayer. We thought praying was all about asking God to rearrange life or the world to our specifications: "O God, help me pass my driving test" etc. But deeper prayer involves a journey towards knowing our true selves. And it usually turns out that the "real me" is more elusive than we had thought.

Our knowledge of ourselves is partial—we may entertain all sorts of illusions about ourselves. A Benedictine monk once suggested to me that Christianity is "three-fifths self-knowledge". An exaggeration, perhaps, but the Bible lends support to that view. There is One—i.e. God—who reads human hearts, who knows us better than we know ourselves. Consider the teaching of Jesus on prayer, "Don't be like the hypocrites" (Matthew 6:5). The Greek word for "hypocrite" means "actor", so: "no pretending, no play-acting"!

With those words Jesus may have had in mind the Pharisees (a devout Jewish sect of his day), but we all acquire images of ourselves, partly manufactured by us, partly projected on to us by others. As Lewis says, what I call "myself" . . . is a "dramatic construction", a collection of our memories, glimpses in the mirror, people's expectations of us and our attempts to live up to them, and much more besides. Who is the real me?

Lewis suggests that in prayer, for once, the real "I" tries to speak—or may do so, if our prayer is honest. A parable of Jesus provides a sharp contrast between honesty and hypocrisy (i.e. self-delusion) in prayer (Luke 18:9–14). The prayer of one man, a Pharisee, expresses how he saw himself, other people and God. The parable implies that a skewed picture of ourselves leads to a skewed picture both of other people and of God:

> "God, I thank you that I am not like other people . . . I fast twice
> a week; I give a tenth of all I possess."

Five "I"s in one short prayer! Our prayers easily become ego-filled. Even if we don't verbalize such thoughts, they're often there. Contrast the other man—a "tax- collector", that is, a man hated as a collaborator with the occupying Roman forces. Here is someone whose prayer showed he had no illusions about himself: "God, be merciful to me, a sinner." This parable reflects the Bible's upside-down world. It's the devout, religious man who's not really engaging with God; the "sinner" presents himself to God just as he is.

There is an honest-to-God character about most biblical prayers. But there are evasive responses to God as well, beginning with Adam and Eve. First, they hide (Genesis 3:8–10), and then the blame-game begins, the man blaming the woman, the woman blaming the serpent (verses 11–13). Nervous evasion and blaming someone else, the Bible seems to suggest, is our default position before God. It's not a promising start to prayer.

The Bible's upside-down world continues. Apart from Adam's reply to God's question "Where are you?", the first words addressed to God in the Bible come from Cain, who has been described as "the world's first murderer". After killing his brother Abel, Cain

> . . . said to the Lord, "My punishment is greater than I can bear! Today you have driven me away from the soil and I shall be hidden from your face . . . "
>
> *Genesis 4:13,14a*

Cain goes away "from the presence of the Lord" (verse 16), but not beyond God's reach, because God makes arrangements for Cain's protection (verse 15). "Hope is possible . . . No one, not even the first murderer, stands outside God's grace."[2]

Other responses to God in the Bible are peppered by protests, questions and doubts. After the disastrous end to God's first attempt to create a world, God tries again (Genesis 12:1–8), and this time a human being (Abraham) seems to be listening. At first, Abraham says not a word to God, just silently does what God has told him to do (Genesis 12:4). But then the doubts begin. God has promised him a son and land. The scenario for both looks deeply unpromising, as is often the way with God's promises in the Bible. At this stage, Abraham has only questions:

---

[2] Michael E. W. Thompson, *I Have Heard Your Prayer: The Old Testament and Prayer* (Peterborough: Epworth Press, 1996), p. 13. (Thompson's book is a valuable, wide-ranging survey.)

"Lord God, what can you give me, seeing that I am childless?"

Genesis 15:2

"Lord God, how can I be sure … ?"

Genesis 15:8

Protests and questions to God come thick and fast not only when God makes promises, but also when God gives people breathtakingly difficult tasks. In the Bible's next book, Exodus, God commissions Moses to go to King Pharaoh of Egypt to demand the release of the Hebrew slaves, and Moses plies God with no less than five reasons for not going (Exodus 3:11,13; 4:1,10,13). The protests to God continue with the prophets: Jeremiah, "I'm too young" (Jeremiah 1:6); Jonah, "I have a boat to catch …" (Jonah 1:3). They run on into the New Testament: Zechariah, father of John the Baptist, "How will I know that this is so? … I am an old man …" (Luke 1:18); even Mary, mother of Jesus, asks, "How can this be, since I am a virgin?" (Luke 1:34); Ananias, called by God to go to the terrifying Saul of Tarsus, "Lord, I have heard from many about this man …" (Acts 9:13).

There is another kind of honesty in the Bible. It occurs in the Old Testament, but not in the New. Bargaining with God begins with Jacob:

"If God will be with me … and will give me bread to eat and clothing to wear … then the Lord shall be my God."

Genesis 28:20–21

Most of us will recognize this kind of prayer ("I will if you will …"). After being away for weeks we turn up at church the Sunday before, say, an important exam: "I'll be a better person in future, if … ".[3] By contrast, the prayer of Jesus in Gethsemane the night before he died, though it begins

---

[3]   It is possible that Old Testament prayers which read like an attempt to bargain with God should be understood as vows which are made in confident anticipation of God's response. On this, see the paragraph at the end of this chapter on "the Old Testament in relation to the New".

with an honest request: "Remove this cup from me . . . " continues "not my will but yours be done" (Luke 22:42).

So prayers of protest and questions are not necessarily a juvenile or primitive stage of prayer which the Bible moves beyond. "Honest to God" seems to be the golden rule. Talking to the Creator of all things like this is apparently—OK! This upside-down biblical world conveys a challenge: unlike most human beings in authority, God prefers a blunt, no-holds-barred conversation with the real me, not a hypocrite or a confected substitute masquerading as the real me. Staying awake matters, too—better than being fast asleep, like Eli (at first) and the disciples of Jesus in Gethsemane (1 Samuel 3:1–9; Mark 14:37–40).

Yet evasions, questions and protests are not the whole picture. There are also *iconic* responses, when the real person stands up to be counted: Moses at the burning bush, "Here I am" (Exodus 3:4); Samuel in the Temple, "Speak, for your servant is listening" (1 Samuel 3:10); Isaiah in the Temple, "Here am I; send me" (Isaiah 6:8). In the New Testament Mary's response to the angel Gabriel has become the paradigm of all Christian responses:

> "Here am I, the servant of the Lord. Let it be with me according to your word."
>
> *Luke 1:38*

"Here I am" may sound straightforward enough, like a child at school answering as the register is called. Like an adult in church, we're either there or not there—present in body, if not always in mind. God is always present to us, but we may be spiritually and emotionally all over the place. But even if we're only half-present before the God who reads our hearts and invites our response, we might wonder what we are letting ourselves in for in responding to God. Yet the Bible consistently promises that the God who calls has the secret of life.

And when our responses are not forthcoming? What if people are simply impervious to God's call? God's call is universal, leaving no one out. But sometimes people will not or cannot respond. Human unbelief can be an unfathomable mystery, and we would be wise to refrain from making judgements about who has or hasn't responded to God, since we, unlike God, can't read human hearts.

Even so, there are stark warnings in the Bible about the consequences of ignoring God's call. If we persist, human hearts begin to "harden"—becoming, for example, increasingly impervious to human suffering. There is another consequence: human hearts are "darkened"; our capacity to distinguish truth from untruth diminishes. (That kind of darkness, says Paul, is one of the results of our idolatries, Romans 1:21.)

But God—the real God—does not "get the hump" when people ignore him. Some passages in the Bible might seem to imply that God is touchy, easily taking offence. That cannot be so. The Bible's climax comes near the end: "God is love" (1 John 4:7). That is the golden thread running all the way through. Even in the darkness we bring upon ourselves, prayer is still possible. (Psalm 107:10–22 provides two striking examples.)

Finally, we conclude this brief survey of honest-to-God responses in the Bible by noting a few of the most significant and powerful. There are three in the Old Testament. Jacob moves from bargaining with God at Bethel to wrestling with God at Peniel (Genesis 28 and 32); Job—enigmatic though the ending of this book is—moves from shouting at God to confessing " . . . now I see you with my own eyes" (Job 42:5); Elijah finds God, not in the wind, earthquake or fire, as Israel had in the past, but in a still, small voice (1 Kings 19:12,13).

In the New Testament there are two. A once-fiercely zealous Paul who now prays for Gentiles has clearly come to a new understanding of God. Most significant of all, the cross of Jesus does away with inherited images of God for disciples who venture on the way of the cross: no fire from heaven or legions of angels putting sinners in their place (Luke 9:54–5; Matthew 26:53). Through the darkness of Jesus' own God-forsakenness (e.g. Mark 15:34) comes the revelation of the God of Abraham as "the God and Father of our Lord Jesus Christ".

These biblical testimonies all suggest that our journey towards the real God may be costly; but it is ultimately transforming and infinitely worthwhile. That brings us to the other half of Lewis' "prayer before all prayers": "*May it be the real Thou that I speak to.*"

Locating the real God

Just as we create false images of ourselves, so we create false images and ideas of God. The roots of these can be complex and various: early experience of a tyrannical or abusive parent, Christian teaching we misunderstood or which was wrong anyway, an unhelpful church—these all may distort our understanding of God. All this quite apart from our own conscience and moral awareness. So a fundamental question is this: to whom, really, are we praying? This is a question which applies to everyone. It may apply especially to Christians, since we, too, create our own images—idols—of God. Religious people are especially prone to this. Again, how judgemental we are is a crucial test (Matthew 7:1, quoted in the previous chapter).

But for some there will be an even more fundamental question: is there a God at all? What's the point of praying if there isn't a God to pray to in the first place? The reality (a better word than "existence") of God can't be proved or disproved. A recent, feisty book about God, however, suggests that, if atheists are serious about evidence for and against God, they should try—really try—to pray.[4]

In response, we may note two kinds of questions in the Psalms. The first comes from the sceptic: "Where is your God?" But does he really want an answer? The way the question is framed might suggest that he thinks he knows the answer anyway. The second kind of question in the Psalms comes from someone who really does want an answer—and is already praying: "Where are you, God?" Here the questioner seems to imply "I know you're really there, even though it doesn't look like it." Or else, perhaps, "I'm not sure you're there—but sometimes I wish you were."

A good place to start in the Bible in our quest for the real God is God's mysterious self-introduction to Moses. The strange name of God in Exodus 3:14 is usually translated as "I am who I am" or "I will be what I will be." This is such an important text. The mysterious, elusive Reality, infinitely beyond us and intimately near, is the One to whom we

---

[4]   David Bentley Hart, *The Experience of God: Being, Consciousness, Bliss* (New Haven, CT: Yale University Press, 2013), p. 327.

pray. With this God of Israel ("the Lord", as this God is called in the Old Testament),[5] no god can compare—as the book of Psalms insists again and again.

In the Bible the existence of God (and gods) is taken for granted. The Bible's emphasis falls on the presence (or, occasionally, absence) of God, but never God's non-existence. So rather than begin with the question "Does God exist?", we start with the idea—or the experience—of a Presence. The poet William Wordsworth, though not yet a Christian, in his poem "Lines Composed Above Tintern Abbey" expressed it like this:

> I have felt
> A presence . . . sense sublime
> Of something far more deeply interfused,
> Whose dwelling is the light of setting suns . . .

If not a setting sun, an experience of human love, as in the arrival of a new-born baby, or a quiet country church, or inspirational music might become a religious experience. Such experiences do not "prove" the existence of God, but they may convey a sense of a presence, or a sense of a mysterious "something more" to life. In such experiences, we are on the threshold of prayer. Growing in prayer can make us more aware of that presence.

The Bible assumes the presence of God from the beginning:

> The Spirit of God swept over the face of the waters.
>
> *Genesis 1:2*

This God is a God of surprises, showing up, unannounced and unexpected, to Abraham, (Genesis 12:7; 15:1; 17:1), to Isaac (Genesis 26:24) and to Jacob (Genesis 28:13). In fact, God shows up all over the place—even to Jewish exiles in pagan Babylon. That is the background both to the question in Isaiah:

---

[5]   Psalm 68:4 "The Lord is his name . . . " echoes the tradition which goes back to the story of the burning bush (Exodus 3:1–15), in which Moses asks God his name and receives the mysterious reply (v. 14) "I am that I am."

Why do you say, O Jacob . . . "My way is hidden from the Lord"?

Isaiah 40:27

and to the affirmation which follows:

Have you not known . . . ? The Lord is the everlasting God . . .

verse 28

(The rest of Isaiah 40 and much of Isaiah 40–55 are an inspirational vision of the real God.) Someone once remarked, "You can't keep a good God down". In the Bible, that seems to apply even when (or especially when?) things are really bad.

So the phrase "always and everywhere" summarizes well the presence of God in the Bible. Devout people in the Bible sometimes feel—deeply and keenly—the absence of God, but God is still present, even in the darkness. No one earns or deserves this presence. In Jacob's case, quite the opposite. After deceiving his aged, blind father and his older brother Esau, he deserved no favours at all from whatever God there might be. Yet God called and blessed even this deceiver (Genesis 27 and 28:10–17). That isn't the only surprise in the Bible. Contrary to some religious practices of the time, no one conjures up the presence of the real God by a special technique or incantation. God is simply there—always and everywhere.

It's as if the world is "haunted" by God, a reality mysteriously reticent and even elusive. But if the real God doesn't coerce or impose his will on humans, the Bible tends to portray God as *persistent*. Persistence is often a characteristic of human beings who love—especially those who love passionately. What one of the Psalms says about the divine presence the whole Bible illustrates:

You hem me in, behind and before,
and lay your hand upon me . . .
Where can I go from your spirit?
Or where can I flee from your presence?

Psalm 139:5,7

This is fundamental to the biblical understanding of God and of prayer. Yet a cautionary note is sounded as well. Human beings should not take God's presence for granted:

> Seek the Lord while he may be found,
> Call upon him while he is near.
>
> *Isaiah 55:6*

The prophet Amos envisages what seems to be a point of no return: the time is coming when "they shall run to and fro, seeking the word of the Lord, but they shall not find it" (Amos 8:12). Prophetic warnings were urgent; no one should presume.

The overall biblical picture, however, is one of hope: whenever and wherever desperate people "cry out" to God, God is there for them. And yet—as the Bible also recognizes—the ever-present God can be experienced as absent—or deaf, a subject to which we now turn.

The God who hears—or does he?

Despite the description of God in the Psalms as "hearer of prayer" (Psalm 65:2), it is not always obvious that God hears prayers. The desperate mother of a child suffering from Hurler syndrome—gargoylism—found herself one evening alone in an empty church. Angrily, she muttered to God, "Damn you, you don't exist, but I hate you." She burst into tears and began to shout: "All right, if you do exist show me a way out. For a start, what the hell am I to do next?"

Experiences like this are not uncommon. The problems of evil and of suffering prompt anguished, angry prayers, and the doubt is never far away: "Is anyone really there?" Biblical writers, as in the Book of Job, raise their doubts. "Unanswered" prayers have been a problem in every age to those who pray. In the story recounted above, the mother, later that evening, read about a Sue Ryder Home for Concentration Camp Victims, and went to help for a week. The experience renewed her faith—and her ability to help others.[6]

Experience of the apparent absence of God is a fact of life and may last a long time—even, or especially for deeply religious people. The counsel of the Psalmist is simply to "hang on", or, put more positively, "Wait for the Lord" (e.g. Psalm 27:14). That waiting, however long, is never a waste of time.

According to the Bible, God hears because God is never out of earshot. Whatever our experience, there is a Reality encompassing us which is a gracious, compassionate "You", not a detached, bureaucratic "It". When we pray, our prayers are not hitting a blank wall. There are no limits to God's "hearing": no boundaries set to the places or the people with whom God communicates and who communicate with God. The people to whom God responded in Psalm 107 could have been anywhere.

God's "hearing" is not confined to hearing explicit, spoken prayers. God hears the cries of suffering Hebrew slaves (Exodus 2:23–4). Does this mean God's hearing is selective—Hebrews only? It appears not. God heard the child Ishmael crying (Genesis 21:17), and Ishmael was the founding father of the nation of Midian. Balaam (Numbers 22–4) is clearly not an Israelite, yet God speaks with him, and he with God. God's hearing also has a bias to the poor. One verse has a special edge to it: God hears not just "the harvesters", but also their wages (James 5:4).

Biblical details such as these raise searching questions about twenty-first century refugees, and the millions more *in extremis*. Yet we might try imagining a world in which no prayers were offered and in which God nudged no one towards compassionate action: a world without religion, including the churches, a world without the UN and other humanitarian agencies. The Bible gives us a picture of a universal Creator *at work*—particularly in human minds and hearts.

The "bottom line" in the Bible, with all its unflinching realism, is that "the Lord is near" (e.g. Psalm 145:18; Philippians 4:5). This utterly real God, despite appearances to the contrary, is "a hearer of prayer". With such language,

---

6   Mary Craig, *Blessings* (London: Hodder & Stoughton and Morrow, 1979), recounted by Cyril Rodd in *The Book of Job* (Peterborough: Epworth Press, 1990), p. 108.

it is saying something profoundly important about that all-encompassing Reality who is the ultimate ground and direction of all our praying.

Conclusion

The two journeys—towards our real selves and the real God—are really one. In the process, there will be protests, doubts and questions in plenty. They are part of the Bible's picture of honest, uninhibited prayer. In this picture, two characteristics of God stand out. One is the persistent, often unexpected presence of God *and* apparent absences prompting the question "Where are you, God?" And the other: God is a hearer of prayer, always near. But in all the light, shade and darkness of this panorama of prayer, there is an iconic response to be made: "Here am I."

A brief aside: The Old Testament in relation to the New

In what follows I draw on the perceptive, sensitive reflections of an Old Testament scholar writing just over a hundred years ago. Followers of Christ, he suggests, are bound to question certain features of Old Testament prayers. He goes on to list: vindictiveness towards enemies; desires for purely material goods (with no clear reference to their spiritual value); bargaining with God, and an "exaggerated self-depreciation or self-assertiveness towards God".

Yet the devotion of the Old Testament is genuine. It can't be caricatured as "legalistic"; it agrees with the New Testament that the effectiveness of prayers doesn't depend on their length, or on whether we offer gifts to God with our prayers. "Prayer can be both genuine and exalted", even if nothing is known of Jesus; the people of the Old Testament "could never have prayed as they did unless they had learnt how to approach God in the true spirit of the son at home in his Father's house".[7]

---

[7]   W. F. Lofthouse, "Prayer in the Old Testament", in *Concerning Prayer* (London: Macmillan & Co Ltd, 1916), pp. 41–65, quotations taken from pp. 59, 60, 61 and 65.

Yet prayer in the New Testament is in the "name" of Christ: that is, the one praying takes up the position and attitude of Christ both to the world and to God.

Prayer

Mysterious God, before you I have nowhere to hide. I have many questions, but let me neither hide nor pretend. Break through my doubts, my questions, my anger and, whether you seem present or absent, help me to trust and to love.

For reflection and discussion

1. Have your own prayers sometimes been as protesting, angry or questioning as those of the Bible?
2. Reflect on or share experiences of what you believed was the presence of God.
3. In what ways can Old Testament prayers and references to prayer enrich our own prayers and practice of prayer?

5

Jesus and his prayer

He taught them . . . Pray then in this way:
  "Our Father in heaven,
  hallowed be your name . . . ,"

Matthew 5:2; 6:9

God has sent the Spirit of his Son into our hearts, crying, "Abba,
Father!"

Galatians 4:6

In the last two chapters, I have suggested that the Bible's starting-point on prayer is not our own prayers, but God's call of love—God's own prayer for his creation, symbolized by the rainbow and God's "outstretched hands" (Isaiah 65:2) to us all. But God, it seems, doesn't go in for monologues or megaphones. Instead, from Abraham onwards, God has drawn humankind into a conversation in which what counts most is honesty; protests, questions, doubts are all "allowed". ("Pray as you can, not as you can't.") Angry cries or puzzled protests to God are better than giving up in despair or not responding at all.

In this chapter, we focus on Jesus, because for Christians Jesus is the heart and the fulfilment of all that the Bible teaches about prayer. He is the supreme practitioner and teacher of prayer. But he is also much more than that. In Jesus God's call to us and our human response come together.[1] He helps us to pray, not only by his teaching and practice, but

---

[1]   This is part of what Christian faith means by its claim that Jesus is fully human and fully divine.

by leading us, through God's Holy Spirit in our hearts, into the very life and heart of God.

In this chapter we shall look at

- the Lord's Prayer—what it meant and came to mean
- how Jesus' own prayer in "heaven" enables our prayers
- the disciples' journey to the cross, and their transformation.

The Lord's Prayer: Does familiarity breed staleness?

The Lord's Prayer is easy to say. It is much harder to mean the words, and harder still to live them. Perhaps we should say the Lord's Prayer more slowly and more often. The language is Jewish, full of Old Testament resonances, and that is to be expected, since Jesus was a Jew. But Jesus by his life, death and resurrection transformed his disciples' understanding of the prayer he gave them.[2]

Our Father in heaven. The pronouns "I", "me" and "my" occur nowhere in this prayer. There is only "our", "us" and "we". "We" can be thought of as a local congregation, the universal Church, or the whole of humankind. This is a prayer which embraces potentially everyone. Not all people can or will want to call God "Father", but Christians, whether in private or in a church, say this prayer with many and on behalf of all. Otherwise, the word "our" can be exclusive and divisive—as in the expressions "our church", "our country", "our God". But here we say "Our Father", not to exclude anyone but in glad acknowledgement that it is God, not we, who has created the warm, intimate relationship implied by "Our Father".

"Father" doesn't mean God is masculine; that would be idolatry—thinking that the image and reality of God are one and the same. Precious though the image "father" is, no word we utter about God, even "father", can adequately express or describe the mystery of God. It's true that

---

[2]   There are two versions of the Lord's Prayer in the New Testament (Matthew 6:9–13 and Luke 11:2–4). The Church, in practice, prays and teaches Matthew's version, except for "as we forgive", which comes from Luke. (Matthew has "as we have forgiven".)

the image of father originated in a patriarchal culture. Yet in the Old Testament there is a deeper, warmer sense in which God was the "father" of his people; God loved them and cared for them.

The Bible teaches that God is beyond "male" and "female" and yet includes them: God made humans, *male and female, in God's own image* (Genesis 1:26–7). Just as important, to call Jesus Son of God and image (*ikon*) of God (e.g. John 1:18; 2 Corinthians 4:4) doesn't make God masculine. The parable of the prodigal son—perhaps more appropriately called "the parable of the Loving Father"—portrays a father whose running, no doubt with robes hitched up, to meet his wastrel of a son, was anything but patriarchal.

Jesus did not invent this way of addressing God. Isaiah 64:8 is clear enough: "Yet, Lord, you are our father." But in the New Testament God is more specifically praised as "the God and Father of our Lord Jesus Christ". The coming of "the Son" helps us see the Father more clearly, making possible a relationship which was not possible before. The first Christians traced back to Jesus the Aramaic word *abba* (Mark 14:36), as two verses in Paul's letters show (Galatians 4:6; Romans 8:15). *Abba* denoted warmth and intimacy, but not excluding authority. It was a word used by adults as well as children, so it's debatable whether the English "Daddy" is the right translation.

The prayer speaks of "our Father *in heaven*". But what does that mean? The Old Testament Psalms claim that God "is in the heavens" (e.g. Psalm 115:3), unlike pagan idols, visibly rooted in one town or city. By contrast, a greater abode for God than the vast skies above could hardly be imagined. In the Bible, "heaven" and "earth" frequently go together—as in this prayer. God created them both (Genesis 1:1). But "heaven" in the Bible is more than the skies above. It is "the unapproachable and incomprehensible part of creation" (Karl Barth), a reminder that there is more to the world than meets the eye. Heaven is neither far away nor a place in the same way that earth is. It is a reality above and beyond, within and around us, a reality in which past, present and future exist as one whole.

Hallowed be your name. Old Testament language continues in the petitions which follow about God's name, God's kingdom and God's will. The "name" goes with "our Father". To pray that it be hallowed is to pray that everyone everywhere may acknowledge and embrace the loving reality of God.

Sadly, the word "God" for many people today has bad or misleading associations and memories—from childhood, from school assemblies, and even from church. (Churches and Christians can be amongst the worst offenders in our misuse of the word "God".) In the Bible, a name often denoted a person's character, and in the case of a god, sometimes the god's purpose and power. In the story of the burning bush, God gives a mysterious answer to Moses' request for God's name. The NRSV gives three translations—all in capitals:

> I AM WHO I AM, *or I AM WHAT I AM, or I WILL BE WHAT I WILL BE*
>
> *Exodus 3:14*

We noted in the last chapter how important this verse is. It suggests that God can't be defined or pinned down. Yet God is "holy": God will be what God is always and everywhere—in Old Testament language, righteous, loving and faithful.[3] In the New Testament, the name of Jesus is virtually identified with God's name (Philippians 2:5–11; cf. John 17:6).

Your kingdom come, your will be done. Like God's name, God's kingdom was and is contested and challenged in the world. In our day, world hunger, nuclear deterrents and nations torn by violence seem to deny the sovereignty of God. Ancient Israel, too, knew that God's kingdom was not obvious—as Psalm 94 shows:

> How long shall the wicked exult?
>
> *verse 3b*

and yet,

> The Lord is King
>
> *e.g. Psalms 93 and 95–99*

---

[3] Psalms 145:8 and 9 are two of many verses in the Old Testament which express God's character. (Cf. Psalm 86:15.)

Jesus transformed his disciples' understanding of God's kingdom through his teaching, his mission to outsiders and his healing power, including the casting out of demons (Luke 11:20). Even his shameful death was *the* revelation of God's kingdom—a victory, in spite of all appearances to the contrary. Jesus was also remembered as doing the will of his Father to the very end—as his prayer in Gethsemane shows:

> Your will, not mine be done.
>
> *Mark 14:36*

All this means that, in the first part of the Lord's Prayer, we are setting our lives in a certain direction: towards God. The Lord's Prayer begins with self-denial. This is not how we, left to ourselves, would begin our prayers! Here it is God first—and this determines how we pray the rest of this prayer.

Give us today our daily bread recalls the miracle of the manna in the wilderness, when God fed a people who complained to Moses that they were in danger of dying of starvation (Exodus 16). The manna couldn't be stockpiled; it was for each day. So, first, the prayer means exactly what it says: give us what we need each day. And we are praying here not just for ourselves, but also with and for the many people in the world who are starving. A story told more than any other in the Gospels is that of Jesus miraculously feeding hungry crowds (e.g. Mark 6:30–44; 8:1–10).

The feeding miracles pre-figure another "feeding": the Last Supper. The one who "gave thanks, broke ... and gave ... ". The meal anticipated his self-giving: "this is my body" (Mark 6:41; 14:22). So "give us this day ..." refers to more than what we eat. Just as Psalm 105 describes the food God gave Israel in the wilderness as "food from heaven" (verse 40), so Christians remember Jesus as "the Bread of Life" (John 6:35,48). Human beings do not live by bread alone; there are even more important things to ask God for.

Forgive ... as we forgive contrasts sharply with many prayers from the wider Greek and Roman world of Jesus' day, such as the curses directed at rivals in business or in love. But there are Jewish parallels; Ecclesiasticus 28:2 in the Apocrypha is very similar.

Does "forgive as we forgive" mean God won't forgive us unless we do so? It might sound like that. But it's truer to say that God *can't* forgive if we don't; how can the God who is love forgive us if we close our hearts to others—as when we judge people uncharitably? Jesus' own prayer as he was crucified takes forgiveness to a new level:

> Father, forgive them; for they do not know what they are doing.
>
> *Luke 23:34*[4]

This prayer doesn't mean that Jesus had to die before God could forgive, as if a price had to be paid. But his death was a supreme act of intercession, "bridging" earth and heaven. (On this theme, see the next section below and Chapter 6.)

Lead us not into temptation (or *Do not bring us to the time of trial*), *but deliver us from evil.* The Greek word here (*peirasmos*) can mean either "temptation" or "test", but in the Bible it usually refers to a specific happening. (The modern version assumes that.) But who does the tempting or testing? The letter of James is very clear:

> No one when tempted should say, "I am being tempted by God";
> for God cannot be tempted by evil and he himself tempts no one.
> But one is tempted by one's own desire ...
>
> *James 1:13,14a*

The Bible seems to say that two forces are at work: God allows us to be tested, but it is Satan who "tempts". The Gospels say that the Spirit "led" (or in Mark, "drove") Jesus into the wilderness, but it was Satan who tempted him (Matthew 4:1; Mark 1:12; Luke 4:1). Many Christians today find it difficult to believe in a personal "devil". Yet the language of the Bible about the power of evil is often expressed in personal images,

---

[4]   Some ancient manuscripts do not have Luke 23:34. But i) Luke's fondness for parallels between Jesus and his apostles in his Gospel and ii) in Acts, his second volume, Stephen's prayer for forgiveness for his persecutors (Acts 7:60), suggest that this prayer of Jesus is part of the original Gospel.

and that language is always stark and realistic. We easily underestimate the reality of evil.

Jesus' own temptations show what the last two petitions of the Lord's Prayer meant for him. They meant putting God before bread, power displays and "the kingdoms of this world". They also meant resisting the temptation to turn the tables on God by putting God to the test, as Israel did in the wilderness. (See, e.g. Psalm 95:8–9.) Disciples would later recall Jesus' own testing in Gethsemane: his prayer "Take this cup from me" surely meant "Spare me this test". God did not, but the Church has always believed that God delivered him from evil, including what has been called his "last temptation": "If you are the Son of God, come down from the cross" (Matthew 27:40).

The prayer "Take this cup from me … " went unanswered. The crucifixion was the hour of darkness (e.g. Luke 22:53; 23:44–5) and Jesus died feeling God-forsaken (Matthew 27:46; Mark 15:34). "Deliver(ance) from evil" in this dark hour was far from obvious—until the resurrection, the enduring reality, Christians would say, that God is present even in the darkness of unanswered prayer.

Did Jesus, sinless as he was (Hebrews 4:15), pray the prayer he gave us? We cannot say. But he surely lived it. His entire life was defined by his baptism and his crucifixion: God's name, God's kingdom, God's will before all things. But that wasn't all. Jesus fed the hungry, taught and practised forgiveness, and "was numbered with transgressors" (Luke 22:37; cf. Isaiah 53:12). In praying with and for Israel he lived the prayer which he gave to his disciples.

We can take the Lord's Prayer too lightly. To say and to mean the Lord's Prayer is, as our baptism implies, a commitment to be "crucified with Christ" (Romans 6:1–11), and to live it is the work of a lifetime. Yet this prayer *carries and renews us* because we pray to One who has revealed himself as "our Father". Its final words, added by the early Church, are given a deeper, triumphant significance in the light of Easter. They are words for us to say especially as we kneel before a cross:

> *Yours is the kingdom, the power and the glory, for ever and ever.*
> *Amen.*

With this doxology the Lord's Prayer comes full circle: it begins and ends with God, not ourselves, in glad acknowledgement that through Jesus we enter in a new way into the very life and being of God.

The prayer of Jesus on earth and in heaven

What do we know of Jesus' own practice of prayer? The Gospels are sketchy: he got up very early to pray (Mark 1:35); he prayed by himself (Luke 9:18) in the hills and the wilderness, and, before choosing the twelve, he prayed all night (Luke 6:12). (Several Psalms also refer to praying during the night (e.g. Psalms 63:6; 119:148)—not a bad use of time if we can't sleep.)

We may think praying came easily to Jesus. In John's Gospel, Jesus, in a public prayer, thanks the Father for hearing him, adding " . . . You always hear me . . . " (11:42). A well-known hymn describes Jesus sharing "the silence of eternity" with his Father in the peace and calm of the Galilean hills. But the letter to the Hebrews gives a different picture:

> [Jesus] throughout his earthly life . . . offered up prayers and petitions with loud cries and tears . . .
>
> *Hebrews 5:7*

So maybe the prayer of Jesus in Gethsemane was typical of other prayers he offered to God. Christian faith, after all, affirms that Jesus was truly human, and many saints, past and present, have written of the tears and agony of prayer. Jesus' lament over Jerusalem seems to express God's own prayer:

> Jerusalem, Jerusalem . . . ! How often have I longed to gather your children, as a hen gathers her brood under her wings.
>
> *Luke 13:34*

A later lament is quite explicit about the tears of Jesus (Luke 19:41–2).

But there is one more vital thing to add here. Jesus' entire life and death were his ultimate sacrifice—i.e. prayer—to God. The New Testament portrays this prayer as a bridge between earth and heaven. His prayer in John 17 reads like a prayer begun on earth and continued in heaven. The final blessing of Jesus in Luke's Gospel is carried—translated—into heaven:

> While he was blessing them, he . . . was carried up . . .
>
> *24:51*

Christians have traditionally called this "the atonement": the at-one-ment of "earth" and "heaven", humankind and God.

John's Gospel attributes to the dying Jesus a cry of victory: "It is accomplished!" (19:30): the circle of prayer, drawn by the One who came from and now returns to God, is complete (John 13:1). The life and death of Jesus (including the scars of the cross) become his eternal "intercession" at God's "right hand":

> It is Christ Jesus, who died, yes, who was raised, who is at the right hand of God, who indeed intercedes for us.
>
> *Romans 8:34; cf. Hebrews 7:25*

The imagery here mustn't mislead us: Jesus is no second-in-command, still less a heavenly lobbyist, bringing pressure to bear on a reluctant God. Rather, his prayer—that is, his life and death—means that there is room in the heart of God for us all. That, I think, is the deepest meaning of the words "In my Father's house are many mansions" (John 14:2).

Thus Jesus' eternal prayer is the unseen engine room of the universe— the seedbed of God's new creation. Jesus' own prayer of thanksgiving during his lifetime on earth anticipates our being drawn into the communion of the Father and the Son:

> no one knows the Son but the Father, and no one knows the Father but the Son *and those to whom the Son chooses to reveal him.*
>
> *Luke 10:21–2; cf. Matthew 11:25–7*

"Choose" here doesn't preclude God's call to everyone. (On this, see Chapter 3.) Rather, it means that we do not make ourselves into disciples; only God can do that. In the same way, our praying only really begins with the help of God's Holy Spirit. If our prayers are to avoid the unreality of "hypocrites"—in touch neither with themselves or God—and the "much speaking" of "pagans" (Matthew 6:5,7; Luke 18:11), we need the Spirit to pray to the Father through Jesus Christ our Lord—the "bridge" between earth and heaven (Romans 8, and especially verses 15 and 26–7).

So "through Jesus Christ . . . " is not a sort of pin number to attach to our prayers to make sure they "get through". It expresses *the reality*: we are *enabled* to pray because we are "in Christ". On this crucial foundation, the eternal prayer of Jesus, all Christian prayer stands. But always, we pray as we can, trusting the Spirit to take us deeper into the reality of Christ.

From semi-detached disciples to disciples "in Christ"

What difference did Easter make to the first disciples of Jesus? Did the twelve disciples become people of prayer? The Gospel pictures of them are not very encouraging. In the words of a school report, we might say, "Could do better". Mark gives the bleakest picture. After a promising start, it becomes clear that the disciples are not on Jesus' "wavelength" at all. They seem, at one point, no better than Jesus' opponents: "Are your hearts hardened?" (Mark 8:17; cf. 3:5).

Not surprisingly, in this condition, they struggle to keep up with their leader. Jesus attributes their inability to heal to their failure to pray (9:29). Their failures multiplied. The nearer Jesus comes to his cross, the worse the disciples become. Jesus, in his farewell speech to them, commands: "Keep awake"—i.e. be prayerful (Mark 13:35; Matthew 24:42; Luke 21:36). But they fall asleep (e.g. Mark 14:37). Jesus, however, has prayed for "Simon", and that will make all the difference:

> Simon, Simon, listen! Satan has demanded to sift all of you like wheat, but I have prayed for you that your own faith may not fail; and you, once you have turned back, strengthen your brothers.
>
> *Luke 22:31–2*

It won't be their own inadequate prayers which will carry them through. It will be the prayer of Jesus. But now, alongside this picture of the disciples, we need to place, first, some teaching on prayer in Paul, and second, the distinctive teaching of the Gospel of John.

A verse about prayer in Paul is often mistranslated. He did not write " ... we do not know *how* to pray as we ought" (Romans 8:26-7), but "we do not know *what* to pray ...". We may think we need guidance on how, but there is a deeper problem: *what* to pray. Yet Paul has just highlighted the solution: "the Spirit comes to the aid of our weakness" (verse 26).

How does the Spirit help? Paul's language here is difficult:

> that very Spirit *intercedes ... intercedes for the saints according to the will of God.*
>
> *verses 26b and 27*

In other words, the Spirit carries on where Jesus left off, bridging earth and heaven—only now, at work in human hearts.

So *what* do we pray? Paul's answer is clear; we pray "Abba, Father"— "the prayer of Jesus" (Roman 8:15,29-34; Galatians 4:6). In this way, the relationship of Jesus with God becomes *our* prayer. The Christian is called to life in Christ and in the Spirit, and that is the seedbed of our prayers. Our prayer becomes our life and our life our prayer:

> I appeal to you ... to present your bodies as a living sacrifice, holy and acceptable to God, which is your spiritual worship.
>
> *Romans 12:1*

Only the Spirit's prayer makes possible our "unceasing" prayer (1 Thessalonians 5:17), when living and praying are one and the same. The heart of prayer, in the Christian view, is very simple: it is Jesus and his prayer. "In Christ" we are caught up in his prayer—a prayer which arises from living "in Christ":

> Abide in me as I abide in you ...
>
> *John 15:4*

The theme of abiding in Christ—Paul's language is simply "in Christ" (especially 2 Corinthians 5:17; Galatians 2:20)—is one to which we must return in our final chapter.

In the "Last Discourses" in John, Jesus enlarges on something he says about prayer in Matthew and Luke: "Ask and it will be given to you" (Matthew 7:7; Luke 11:9):

> On that day you will ask nothing of me. Very truly I tell you, if you ask anything of the Father in my name, he will give it to you. Until now you have not asked for anything in my name. Ask and you will receive that your joy may be complete.
>
> *John 16:23–4*

Which "day" is this verse talking about? Probably Easter Day—or Easter *and* Pentecost. From being spectator-disciples, following Jesus and looking at the crucified Jesus "from afar", they now become disciples "*in Christ*": "you in Me and I in you" (John 14:20). (We shall need to return to this theme of praying "in my name"—that is praying "through Jesus Christ our Lord" in Chapter 7, "Asking".)

Even now, for them and all subsequent disciples, the call to perseverance and discipline in prayer remains. But even if Luke's picture of the early church in Acts is somewhat idealized (e.g. Acts 2:42–7), Easter-with-Pentecost transformed their prayers. Now they are "carried" by the eternal prayer of Jesus.

Conclusion

Jesus is more than a teacher and example of prayer, important though that is. He is also iconic in a deeper way. The central claim of Christian faith is that God in Christ draws us into his own "eternal" life through grace and faith. God's grace—his undeserved generosity and forgiveness—calls forth our faith and trust and therefore our prayers. We are enabled to say, from the heart, "Abba, Father". Whatever our failures—past, present and future—in prayer, this is the life-enhancing road to which God calls us. For most of us, the transition from "semi-detached" disciples to "life in

Christ" does not happen overnight. But it is the road along which God invites us. Along this road we learn to live, as well as pray, the prayer which Jesus gave us.

Prayer

Jesus, Son of God, lead me to your Father and my Father, that through you I may receive the life and love for which I was created, and see life, the world and other people with new eyes. Take from my heart and mind every unloving thought about others so that your universal love may find my heart.

For reflection and discussion

1. How may the Lord's Prayer become or continue to be fresh and heartfelt for us?
2. In what ways, if any, are God and other people a problem for you in your praying?
3. Is there a pattern for us and for our prayers in the New Testament's pictures of the disciples before and after the cross and resurrection?

6

The Great Thanksgiving

Grace to you and peace from God our Father and the Lord Jesus
Christ . . . I thank my God through Jesus Christ for all of you . . .

Romans 1:7b–8a

Do not worry about anything, but in everything . . . with
thanksgiving let your requests be made known to God.

Philippians 4:6

The eternal intercession of Jesus is the bridge between humankind and
God, according to the New Testament. Our own prayers "piggyback" on
his: prayer is now offered "through Jesus Christ our Lord". This is not a
Christian "pin number" which ensures our prayers "get through". It's the
Spirit of Jesus, the Holy Spirit, who helps us to pray as Jesus prayed. To put
it another way, God's own prayer—God's call of love—evokes ours. With
that in mind, we shall be exploring in the next four chapters the Christian
response in prayer in the new era created by Jesus. Thanksgiving is the
natural place to start.

Thanking an extravagant God

Imagine our Creator's intent: how to evoke out of primeval clay love,
joy and thankfulness. It would take time! Apart from the millennia of
evolution, *homo sapiens* has turned out to be quite a problem: not so
sapiens at all—and by *sapiens* ("wise") I imply the Bible's understanding
of wisdom: recognizing the reality and presence of our Creator.

There is a mystery here. We can see our Janus-like character even
in little children: innocence, wonder, receptiveness and sheer *joie de*

vivre alongside self-absorption, jealousy, aggression . . . St Paul describes a "grown-up" world darkened by illusion, injustice, broken relationships and—the root of it all—idolatry:

> Though knowing God, they did not honour or give thanks to God.
>
> *Romans 1:21*

Our Creator hoped for thankfulness, and it wasn't there; we grumble at terms and conditions, take for granted so much of what we've been given, or simply don't even notice it's there.

Yet there is so much to be thankful for. The Old Testament is wonderfully world-affirming. Its very first chapter tells us seven times that God saw that the world he was making "was good". How can we not be thankful? The law of Moses pointed the way, prescribing thank-offerings to God (Leviticus 7:12; 22:29). Many of the Psalms do far more, giving heartfelt expression to thanking, blessing and praising God:

> I will bless the Lord at all times,
> His praise shall be continually in my mouth.
>
> *Psalm 34:1*

("Blessing" God means responding gratefully to God for all his blessings to us.)

The Psalmists never tire of telling us: "It is a good thing to give thanks to the Lord" (Psalms 106 and 107:1), who rescues even those who rebel against him (Psalm 107:10–22). From life's beginning on into old age there is cause to thank God (Psalm 71).

The Psalms pose a challenge: how can prayers of thankfulness become thankfulness? It's easy to say prayers of thanks because we know we should. To be grateful to God is a deeper thing altogether. How can thankfulness become a way of life?

The new note of thankfulness in the New Testament is unmistakable. The thanksgivings which permeate Acts, the letters and Revelation are anticipated in all the Gospels. Jesus' own prayer of thanksgiving we noted briefly in the last chapter. Its final sentence expresses the promise that disciples will come to share the experience reflected in this prayer:

> At that time Jesus said, "I thank you, Father, Lord of heaven and earth, because you have hidden these things from the wise and the intelligent and have revealed them to infants; yes, Father, for such was your gracious will. All things have been handed over to me by my Father; and no one knows the Son except the Father, and no one knows the Father except the Son and *anyone to whom the Son chooses to reveal him.*"
>
> *Matthew 11:25–7; Luke's version, 10:21–2, is almost identical*

"The Son's" choice expresses, as we saw in Chapter 3, God's initiative in reaching out to us and making possible our response to him. So already in this prayer there are the seeds of post-Easter thankfulness. They are there, too, in many of Jesus' parables and miracles, including the feeding miracle which anticipates both *the Eucharist* (from the Greek word for thanksgiving, *eucharistia*) of the Church and a "heavenly banquet" (e.g. Mark 6:30–44). God's extraordinary generosity to us all will be clearer still in the light of the cross and resurrection. This prayer foreshadows a "new creation" into which all are invited (2 Corinthians 5:17).

Thankfulness and prayers of thanksgiving are leading themes in Paul's letters. Most of his letters begin with such a prayer. Letter-writers then often did this, thanking the gods for, say, good health or a safe journey. But Paul lifts this literary convention to a new plane:

> Grace to you and peace from God our Father and the Lord Jesus Christ ... I thank God through Jesus Christ for all of you.
>
> *Romans 1:7–8*

Paul's thanksgivings vary. One becomes a prayer for the church (Philippians 1:3,9), another is like a Jewish *berakah* (a blessing) (2 Corinthians 1:3–4). Whatever their style, these letter openings set the tone for what follows: thankfulness for God's grace and love in Christ and for life lived "in Christ". These are themes which course through Paul's writings. (Praise, too, keeps breaking through—more of that in

Chapter 10.) The apostle's language tells all. Thanksgivings "multiply" and "overflow" (2 Corinthians 4:15); a "flood of thanksgiving" will be an important outcome of his great ecumenical project, the famine relief offered by Gentile Christians for Jewish Christians (2 Corinthians 9:11). Thanks and praise permeate many of the Psalms, too, but now there is a new and even greater reason for thanking the God of Israel. Now thankfulness pervades the whole of life:

> . . . give thanks *in all circumstances,* for this is the will of God in
> Christ Jesus for you.
>
> *1 Thessalonians 5:18*

"Laments" and "cries" from the depths—to mention just two forms of Old Testament prayers—continue, as Paul's own experiences show (e.g. 2 Corinthians 1:8). Yet there is also a new note:

> neither height nor depth . . . will be able to separate us from the
> love of God in Christ Jesus our Lord.
>
> *Romans 8:39*

Psalms such as Psalms 34 ("Praise for Deliverance from Trouble") and 116 ("Thanksgiving for Recovery from Illness") shouldn't be overlooked. Yet in the New Testament thankfulness and thanksgiving seem to pop up everywhere:

> . . . whatever you do, in word or deed, do everything in the name
> of the Lord Jesus, giving thanks to God the Father through him.
>
> *Colossians 3:17*

When we recall the social make-up of a typical Christian house-group (women and slaves, for example), this is extraordinary teaching. Such thankfulness is no formality, as Paul's language shows in almost all his letters. It is the "default mode" of Christian prayer (Philippians 4:6; Colossians 4:2).

Thanksgiving for Jesus takes pride of place in the New Testament, but the world-affirming nature of the Old Testament is carried forward into the New:

> ... all things are yours, whether ... the world or life or death or the present or the future—all belong to you, and you belong to Christ, and Christ belongs to God.
>
> *1 Corinthians 3:21b–3*

This is a remarkable statement. The sequence of thought is the key: only because we belong to God and to Christ are all things ours. Life in Christ, Paul implies, enables us to appreciate "all the blessings of this life" even more, not less, as another letter of his illustrates:

> Finally, beloved, whatever is true, whatever is honourable, whatever is just, whatever is pure, whatever is pleasing, whatever is commendable, if there is any excellence and if there is anything worthy of praise, think about these things.
>
> *Philippians 4:8*

Teaching on prayer and the promise of blessing (verses 7 and 9) enclose this very Greek-sounding vision of beauty, truth and goodness.[1]

Another letter, bearing Paul's name but probably by a later disciple of his, continues this theme, perhaps to counter an unbalanced Christian faith which denied the goodness of creation:

> For everything created by God is good, and nothing is to be rejected, provided it is received with thanksgiving; for it is sanctified by God's word and by prayer.
>
> *1 Timothy 4:4–5*

(Other verses in the New Testament which affirm God's good gifts in life include 1 Timothy 6:17 and James 1:17.)

---

[1] Markus Bockmuehl, *The Epistle to the Philippians* (London: A & C Black Ltd., 1997, 4th edition), p. 250.

Thanksgiving and thankfulness are everywhere in the New Testament. But we must go on to ask: where does the message of the cross, of being "crucified with Christ" and "sharing in the sufferings of Christ" fit into all this? The "farewell speech" of Jesus to his disciples leaves them in no doubt about what lies in store for them (Mark 13 and its parallels in Matthew 24 and Luke 21). In his conclusion, Jesus calls them to the kind of persevering prayer which will carry them through (Mark 13:33–7; Luke 21:34–6). Yet even then thankfulness will keep breaking through. In John's version of Jesus' farewell to his disciples, an Easter glory peeps through. Three times Jesus promises that whatever the disciples ask in his name the Father will grant (John 14:13; 15:16 and 16:23). Asking "in the name of Jesus" means reflecting the glory of God (14:13), bearing "fruit that will last" (15:16), and sharing both the pain and joy of God in the world (16:20–24). Paul strikes the same note:

> . . . as sorrowful, yet always rejoicing; as poor, yet making many rich; as having nothing and yet possessing everything.
>
> *2 Corinthians 6:10*

What does all this mean in practice?

Neville Ward's *The Use of Praying* gives pride of place to thanking God. If life

> . . . is lived thankfully it is well on the way to becoming a holy thing . . . Christianity is a religion of happiness. It wants all men [*sic*] to be happy, to be able to live thankfully instead of resentfully.[2]

In a similar vein, William Temple wrote:

> It is probable that in most of us the spiritual life is impoverished and stunted because we give so little place to gratitude. It is more important to thank God for blessings received than to pray for them beforehand.[3]

---

[2]   Neville Ward, *The Use of Praying* (London: Epworth Press, 1967), p. 20.

[3]   Quoted in *Spirit Level* (Peterborough: Methodist Publishing House, 1992), p. 71.

So where do we begin? C. S. Lewis recommended that we start by thanking God for something down-to-earth: whatever comes first to mind or to hand. Pray as you can. But in all and above all, give thanks for Jesus.

The God who runs to meet us—Confessing

Several words which are prominent in the Bible are widely misunderstood these days. People find words such as "sin" and "repentance" unhelpful and off-putting. "Confession" may be another. It can seem like grovelling before God, as if the first thing to do in church is to spell out to God all the reasons why we don't deserve to be there at all. That is true, but is confession the best place to start?

The New Testament can help us understand confession in a more positive way. It means getting real about ourselves and the world before God and "abandoning the desire to be right".[4] That is easier said than done. We need to hear some good news if we are to receive the faith and courage to do that.

A good place to begin is a prayer of confession *which was interrupted.* In Jesus' parable, the Prodigal Son, the returning "prodigal" had rehearsed his prayer whilst he was still a long way from home. Before he could even get that far, his father had spotted him, "still a long way off". The returning son began the lines he had rehearsed:

> Father, I have sinned against heaven and before you; I am no longer worthy to be called your son . . .
>
> *Luke 15:21*

But that was as far as he got. The rest of the speech which he had planned to say—" . . . treat me like one of your hired hands" (verse 19)—remained unsaid. His father had already embraced and kissed his returning son, and his instructions for a party interrupted the carefully prepared confession (verses 20,22).

---

4   Ward, *The Use of Praying*, p. 41.

It's been said that if we take one step towards God, God will take ten steps towards us. But the story the New Testament tells is more wonderful even than that: God set off looking for us before we had even started. Karl Barth, perhaps the twentieth century's greatest theologian, wrote of God's coming into the world in Christ as a journey, like that of the prodigal, "into the far country": "the Father" coming to find his children.

What does the prodigal son's interrupted prayer tell us about the New Testament's understanding of the prayer of confession? The poet and theologian Samuel Coleridge provides the key:

> Christianity is not so much the gift of forgiveness to those who repent, but the gift of repentance to those who sin.

The story of Zacchaeus in Luke's Gospel illustrates the point well. When did Zacchaeus turn from curiosity about Jesus to repentance—i.e. a real change of heart and mind? Probably when Jesus told him "I must stay at your house today" (Luke 19:5). By all the religious and moral standards of the time, that was an extraordinary, shocking thing to say. A meal with Zacchaeus—not just any old "tax collector", but the godfather of them all (verse 2)! (A modern equivalent would be a Mafia boss or a gangmaster.)

What follows (verse 8) sounds like Zacchaeus' prayer of confession:

> Half of my possessions, Lord, I will give to the poor, and if I have defrauded anyone of anything, I will pay him back four times as much.

This was Zacchaeus' moment of truth. It cost him, but he gladly embraced it, as Jesus' response showed:

> Today salvation has come to this house, because he too is a son of Abraham.
>
> *verse 9*

Confession isn't so much the condition for coming to God, but the result of God finding us. That is when we begin to find ourselves—ourselves as the persons God intended us to be. This helps to explain why there is another confession in the New Testament, and, like the confessions of the returning son and of Zacchaeus, it is life-changing: our confession of Christ. This is how Paul puts it:

> ... if you confess with your lips that Jesus is Lord and believe in your heart that God raised him from the dead, you will be saved.
>
> *Romans 10:9*

Paul is echoing a passage from Deuteronomy (30:12–14) in which our "mouths" and "hearts" go together. This is a heartfelt confession: confessing Christ means a shift in our life's centre of gravity; that centre now is Christ.

But we still, of course, have sins to confess. That's why disciples continue to pray "Forgive us our sins ... ". It helps to understand what confessing means in practice if we distinguish between "sin" and "sins". "Sin" is a difficult word, but, basically, it means: being alienated from our True Centre—God, *and* our deepest self. There are usually social consequences: being at odds with other people as well. Christian tradition, misleadingly, calls this universal condition "original sin".

Through our baptism "into Christ", Paul says (Romans 6:1–11), we "die to sin". Our baptism expresses the real truth about us: our deepest centre is not our sin, but "Christ". And so we start to live as if that's true—because it is. However slowly—and not without setbacks—we begin to receive the grace (i.e. God's power) to fight our "sins" (plural), by, for example, praying the Lord's Prayer each day.

Confessing is basically being honest—getting real before God and—again, not without a struggle!—with each other:

> ... confess your sins to one another ...
>
> *James 5:16; cf. 1 John 1:9*

As with "thanking", so with "confessing", we don't leave the Old Testament behind when we turn to the New. Psalm 51 ("Have mercy on me, O God ... "), traditionally associated with David's murder of Uriah, is the best-known psalm of confession. Today its language may seem "over the top":

> I was born guilty,
> a sinner when my mother conceived me.
>
> *verse 5*

Yet this acknowledgement of "original sin" is a way of recognizing our full membership of a flawed human race, as saints have always known. In the Old Testament, national leaders pray not only for themselves, but for the whole people (Ezra 9:5–15; Nehemiah 1:4–11; 9:6–37; Daniel 9:18). For example, Daniel's intercession for his people is a confession which acknowledges the only possible grounds for forgiveness:

> We do not present our supplication before you on the ground
> of our righteousness, but on the ground of your great mercies.
>
> *Daniel 9:18 (on this prayer see also Chapter 8)*

The Old Testament, like the New, recognizes that we human beings need to confess our failures before our Creator. It's not grovelling; it's starting to get real. But the Old Testament also, like the New, testifies to the reality of God's forgiveness. The book of Leviticus (5:1; 16:21; 26:40) prescribes "sin-offerings", not to earn God's forgiveness, but to realize it (Leviticus 5:13,18). The Letter to the Hebrews argues at length that sin-offerings are no longer needed, because Jesus' offering of himself was "once for all". But we must do justice to the Old Testament. "Thank offerings", reflecting Israel's loyalty and gratitude to God, come before sin and guilt offerings in Leviticus (1–3), and the conviction that God forgives sins was central to Israel's understanding of God:

> There is forgiveness with you, so that you may be revered.
>
> *Psalm 130:4*

In summary, the Christian gospel is the culmination and heart of the Bible's story of love: God's unconditional, undeserved love for us all—the whole of humankind. God in Jesus came into "the far country", living our life and dying our death. This doesn't mean that what the prodigal son had done didn't matter, and he could do the same thing all over again. This is often the risk when someone forgives, as Paul recognized:

"Shall we continue sinning so that God can forgive still more?" (Romans 6:1). But Paul answers his own rhetorical question with a resounding "No!" The Lord's Prayer expresses the new reality: "Our Father . . ." *and* "forgive . . . as we forgive".

There is no such thing as solitary Christianity

Those words spoken to John Wesley remind us that no survey of prayer in the Bible would be balanced or complete if it did not do justice to disciples of Jesus praying and worshipping together. There are great social pressures in "developed" countries to privatize religion. It is politically convenient—and decent, so it is thought—for religion to be a private, individual matter.

The personal nature of prayer in the Bible is not in doubt. But nor is its corporate character. ("Personal" isn't the same as "individual".) The Psalms provide a good template in their combination of individual and corporate prayers. Yet this is more easily said than achieved. A saying of Jesus in Matthew's Gospel is understandably treasured by small congregations:

> For where two or three are gathered in my name, I am there among them.
>
> *Matthew 18:20*

It is preceded by an extraordinary promise:

> Again, truly I tell you, if two of you agree on earth about anything you ask, it will be done for you by my Father in heaven.
>
> *Verse 19*

Agreeing before God is also easier said than done. (I once heard of a tiny congregation where no one was on speaking terms with any of the others!) The scene envisaged here may be one of reconciliation and forgiveness; two people have quarrelled, and a third acts as a mediator, (see Deuteronomy 19:15). Whether that is so or not, the prayers of Jesus' disciples and the quality of their relationships belong closely together.

"There is no such thing as solitary Christianity." Vignettes of the early Christians in the Acts of the Apostles bear this out. Even if Luke has idealized a little, the picture in Acts 2 has a ring of truth: "they devoted themselves . . . to the breaking of bread and prayers" (verse 42). The disciples pray together a little later in the narrative (Acts 4:24–31). The prayer which Luke has recorded—or, perhaps, composed—is reminiscent of the Psalms, particularly in its invitation to God to "look at" the threats of Herod and Pilate (verse 29).

There are more examples in Acts of the early Christians praying together: for guidance (1:24; 13:1–3); when laying hands on people commissioned for service (6:6; 13:1–3; 14:23); in a crisis (12:5,12; 16:25); at emotional farewells (20:36; 21:5). This list is not exhaustive; the point is not the historical accuracy of every detail, but that this is a scriptural (i.e. normative) picture of the Church.

A recurring theme in Acts is the faithful guidance and provision of God. That is the theme of the whole Bible. Yet this needs to be understood in the light of the passion and death of Jesus. At the heart of Christian faith and liturgy is an unanswered prayer. The Son of God in Gethsemane prayed "Take this cup from me . . . " and God did not. Yet God was present in the cross, as the resurrection revealed. And so that darkest night has been gathered up into the thanksgiving prayer of every Eucharist celebrated down the centuries and across the world. (On this, see also Chapter 11.) This brings us to what most Christians have always felt to be the heart of the Church's life of prayer.

Christians give different names to the sharing of bread and wine which constitutes for most the central act of Christian worship. But whether we call it the Lord's Supper, the Mass or Holy Communion isn't the most important thing. What matters is that it places a thanksgiving for Jesus at the heart of the Church's life. That is why it is often called *the* Eucharist; the thanksgiving at the heart of everything. The Greek word *eucharistia* establishes the nature of the principal Christian act of prayer and also the quality of the Christian attitude to life.

This thankfulness, as we saw earlier in this chapter, spread everywhere. It infused their prayers for each other, and it seems to have been the dominant theme of their singing:

> Be thankful. Let the word of Christ dwell in you richly; teach and admonish one another in all wisdom; and with gratitude in your hearts sing psalms, hymns, and spiritual songs to God.
>
> *Colossians 3:15–16; cf. Ephesians 5:19, and*
> *the cameo of an early Christian assembly in which*
> *"each one has a hymn" in 1 Corinthians 14:26*

A note on "speaking in tongues"

"Speaking in tongues" is a form of prayer directed to God. It deserves more discussion than I am able to give it here. In 1 Corinthians 12:10, St Paul recognizes it as a gift of the Spirit, discussing it at length in 1 Corinthians 14. The dramatic picture of Pentecost in Acts 2:1–11, which surely owes something to the author's artistic licence, seems to literalize "tongues".

Whether there are parallels today to that particular experience is uncertain. But whatever the history behind the graphic picture in Acts, its intended meaning is clear. A miracle of communication begins to put into reverse the "curse" of Babel, the mythical origin (Genesis 11:1–9) of humankind's different language and our divisions.

A recent authoritative discussion of speaking in tongues quotes the views of a leading Pentecostalist scholar, Gordon Fee. According to Fee, there is simply no way of knowing whether today's speaking in tongues replicates those of Paul's churches, and the question is probably "irrelevant" anyway. Yet, he concludes, "tongues are directed to God, and Paul holds their private use in high regard".[5]

---

[5]   Anthony C. Thistleton, *The First Epistle to the Corinthians* (Grand Rapids: Eerdmans, 2000), p. 1100.

Conclusion

Prayer in the New Testament has a new centre and a new focus. Disciples pray in Christ, and their prayers are offered in his name. Thanksgiving has a new centre, as so many of the introductions to the New Testament letters show. This new focus, and the command to give thanks "in all circumstances" suggests that thankfulness is now more than thanking God for blessings received, important though that remains. It's the primary root, for individuals and the community, of *a life received and lived*. Christians give thanks, above all, for Jesus, and that is why the Church's central act of worship is called "the Eucharist".

"Confessing", too, has a new centre: it is, first and foremost, a response to good news—as in the parable of the prodigal son. Now, although Christians continue to confess their sins to God and to one another, confessing Christ is centre stage. They are no longer the victims and prisoners of a closed, self-serving system traditionally called "original sin"; they are "in Christ".

Prayer

God and Father of Jesus, have I really heard his gospel? I sometimes think I have to confess my sin if you are ever to forgive me. I find it hard to believe that I am loved—by You, my Creator. Find my heart; still my soul, so that in welcoming You, my whole life may be transformed by thankfulness and praise.

For reflection and discussion

1. The Church's General Thanksgiving expresses thanks to God for "all the blessings of this life", and goes on to give thanks "above all" for Jesus. As with the Lord's Prayer, how may we mean and live what we say?

2. Do you agree with the suggestion—in the light of Jesus' parable—that true confession is the result of hearing good news—i.e. the good news of the gospel?

3. What is our experience of "Holy Communion"—i.e. *the* Thanksgiving?

7

Ask and you will receive?

I call out to you, God, but you do not answer . . .

Job 30:20

Delight in the Lord,
and he will grant you your heart's desire.

Psalm 37:4

Until now you have not asked for anything in my name. Ask and
you will receive . . .

John 16:24

In the little paperback *Children's Letters to God*, there is a section called
"Requests, Reasonable and Otherwise". Amongst the examples, "Eric"
brings to God his wish-list for Christmas: "Dear God, I would like these
things . . .". A list of five items, including a bicycle and a dog, follows. The
letter, however, ends on a note of doubt:

If I can't have all of them, I would like to have most of them.

Another boy clearly thinks there is a limit to what you can pray for:

I never asked for anything before—you can look it up.

Should we grow out of this simple, childlike approach to prayer? After all,
Jesus said "Ask, and you will receive", and "Unless you become like little
children, you will not enter the kingdom of God." To say the least, there
is much confusion and uncertainty about prayers of petition or asking.

Jesus of sick people seeking healing (e.g. Mark 3:11; Matthew 8:29, and many more). The final "cry" (literally, "shout") in Mark and Matthew—the words of Psalm 22:1—is that of Jesus himself:

> My God, my God, why have you forsaken me?
>
> *Mark 15:34; Matthew 27:46*

This, astonishingly, is a prayer from one whom Christians have come to acknowledge as the Son of God. It is not the only prayer of Jesus which comes from the Psalms (see also Luke 23:46). It is a salutary reminder to Christians inclined to be dismissive of the Old Testament that the Old Testament is fulfilled in the New, not left behind. Neat distinctions between Old and New on the subject of prayer cannot easily be made.

Two stories of prayer in the Old Testament are especially powerful. The Book of Job contains perhaps the angriest prayers in the entire Bible. An ordained minister told me once of his angry protests to God as he sat at the bedside of his wife dying very painfully from cancer. In the biblical story, Job is very devout to begin with. Disaster upon disaster descends upon him, to which he responds:

> ... the Lord gave, and the Lord has taken away; blessed be the name of the Lord.
>
> *Job 1:21*

A few chapters later, Job has changed his tune:

> Your hands fashioned and made me;
> And now you turn and destroy me.
>
> *Job 10:8*

There is much more of the same in the chapters which follow, including the verse at the beginning of this chapter. This is exasperated, angry prayer—"*Where is He?*"—despite all the cliché-ridden, pious language of Job's friends.

There are other Old Testament prayers from the depths, such as the strange story of Elijah's flight from Jezebel into the wilderness and from there to Mount Horeb. Elijah is suicidal; that is the reality. It was madness to go "a day's journey into the wilderness" without any provisions at all. He prays for death (1 Kings 19:4), but God, instead, sends an angel to sustain the prophet with food and drink, and on the strength of that he travels to Mount Horeb.

But Elijah's crisis of faith is still not over. On Mount Horeb, the Lord was not in the earthquake, the fire or the wind (verses 11–12), even though, in the past, God had revealed himself to Israel in all these ways. There followed an intense silence ("a still, small voice"), and out of that silence, the word of God (verses 12b–13). "The Lord's puzzling absence was the prelude to his surprising presence."[3] It's as if, when one way of praying goes dead or cold, another, by a way of "unknowing" or of silence may open up for us. Sharing in the silence of God does not make our asking redundant. But it will transform it.

There is much to learn from the Old Testament, especially the Psalms, about prayers of asking. The Psalms seem to say—again and again—two apparently contradictory things: God always hears our prayers, *and* it can often seem that God does not. The first refers to God's character: God's "unfailing love". That is the fundamental reality above, beneath and all around us. The second—that God appears not to be listening—is sometimes our experience, and that is real, too. But our experience will never cancel out the reality of God—hence the Psalms' insistence:

> Commit your way to the Lord;
> Trust in him, and he will act.
>
> *Psalm 37:5*

This same psalm also says something intriguing about what we want—or might not want:

> Delight in the Lord,
> And he will grant you your heart's desire.
>
> *Verse 4*

---

[3]   Robert Davidson, *The Courage to Doubt* (London: SCM Press, 1983), p. 99.

This is both a searching challenge and a remarkable promise. It seems to anticipate a saying of Jesus in the Sermon on the Mount:

> Seek first the kingdom of God ... and all these things will be given to you as well.
>
> *Matthew 6:33*

It will be clear from this section that we do not leave the Old Testament behind when we turn to the New. Rather, the Old is "fulfilled" in the New. We shall find a similar pattern when we turn in the next chapter to the subject of praying for others.

The bottom line

What did people of the ancient world—the Gentile contemporaries of Jesus—pray for? Plenty of evidence has survived. Papyri have been unearthed in Egypt containing magical spells, and the prayers which, people believed, would "activate" the spells. What people prayed for most was health, but other things are high on the list as well: wealth, skill and success at work, success in one's love life, a happy marriage, safe childbirth, emancipation from slavery, safe journeys—all these things feature prominently in ancient prayers.

These prayers weren't simple, as their language often shows. You had to get right (so it was thought) the name of the god to whom you were praying; otherwise, the prayer might not be answered, or the god might take offence. This is why some ancient prayers have long preambles.

And there were so many gods (and goddesses) to choose from. They weren't mutually exclusive—you could pray to more than one, unless, of course, you were a Jew or a Christian. Some scholars have dubbed this period an age of religious anxiety, and if it was, it would be understandable. (What if you missed out a god you should have included?) Altars to "unknown gods" seem to have functioned like a religious insurance policy. Paul observed something very similar at Athens (Acts 17:23).

Occasionally in the New Testament we get a glimpse of this wider religious world. Jesus, in the Sermon on the Mount, criticizes "Gentiles" for thinking that the longer the prayer, the more likely it would be heard (Matthew 6:7). St Paul is aware of the contrast between Christians and other people: for them there are "many gods and many lords", "for us . . . one God . . . one Lord" (1 Corinthians 8:5,6).

It is easy for us to feel superior to all this "pagan" superstition. Yet our own "shopping lists" in prayer often resemble those of the ancient magical papyri. That doesn't mean that our prayers should be so "spiritual" that what is really troubling us never surfaces in our prayers. That is neither honest nor healthy. It's important not to be "sniffy" about prayers of petition, as if mature Christians ought to outgrow them. Yet the saying of Jesus is not the blank cheque it is sometimes taken to be:

> So I say to you, Ask and it will be given you: search and you will find; knock and the door will be opened for you.
>
> *Luke 11:9*

This saying is amplified (so it would seem) in John's Gospel (to which we come in the next section):

> Whatever you ask in my name, this I will do . . .
>
> *John 14:13–4; cf. 15:16; 16:23–4*

The Lord's Prayer points us, as we noted earlier in Chapter 5, in the same direction: God first; his name be hallowed . . . his will be done. . . . In the light of everything that Jesus taught and lived and died for, perhaps we should say: *God himself* is the One we should ask and search for above all else: seek first his kingdom (Matthew 6:33).

If only we had even the tiniest faith, so much could happen:

> Have faith in God. Truly I tell you, if you say to this mountain, "Be taken up and thrown into the sea", and if you do not doubt in your heart, but believe that what you say will come to pass, it will be done for you. So I tell you, whatever you ask for in prayer, believe that you have received it, and it will be yours.
>
> *Mark 11:22–4; cf. Matthew 21:21–2*

I'm sure Jesus did not intend his hearers to take the first part of this teaching literally. The teaching of Jesus contains many hyperboles— striking exaggerations chosen to make a point. But we still need to take his teaching on prayer very seriously. Both Jesus' audience and the Gospels' first readers were living through times of crisis and, for many, oppression and poverty. In such times disciples must trust in God's unwavering faithfulness. Such is that faithfulness that the one who prays can confidently believe that they have already received it even before it arrives.

But more is required of those who pray, as a searching rider to this teaching on prayer shows:

> Whenever you stand praying, forgive, if you have anything against anyone; so that your Father in heaven may also forgive you your trespasses.
>
> *Mark 11:25*

As we saw in an earlier chapter, the Lord's Prayer makes very clear how our being forgiven and our forgiving others cannot be separated. Forgiving other people is the feature of faith "that most perfectly epitomizes God's nature".[4] Its prominence in the teaching of Jesus can hardly be overstated.

What of all those prayers of asking which come most readily to our lips, from "Lord, let me not miss the train" to the much more weighty "Lord, please heal my loved one"? First, praying about our travel plans might or might not trivialize prayer; it depends on what we are doing or where we are going. What we pray about shows up what matters most to us. (What does my panic about missing a train say about me and my priorities?) Paul prayed about his travel plans (e.g. Romans 1:10), as most people did in the ancient world, because travel was arduous and usually dangerous. It was natural for Paul to offer his travel plans to God's providence, since he travelled in the service of the gospel.

---

[4]   James R. Edwards, *The Gospel According to Mark* (Grand Rapids, MI: Eerdmans, 2002), p. 348.

What of more anguished prayer, such as praying for a seriously ill
loved one? A verse in Philippians is a good place to start in thinking
about petitionary prayer in the early churches:

> Do not worry about anything, but in everything by prayer and
> supplication with thanksgiving let your requests be made known
> to God.
>
> *Philippians 4:6*

Such prayer, Paul implies, is an antidote to anxiety and worry. "Worry can
be the delayed symptom of a practical atheism that grows from persistent
neglect of prayer",[5] whereas prayer "with thanksgiving" means God is
already setting us free from our anxiety. Peace, as Paul goes on to say, is
a further result of such prayer:

> The peace of God which surpasses all understanding, will guard
> your hearts and your minds in Christ Jesus.
>
> *Philippians 4:7*

Paul is not talking in Christian clichés here. Nor, I think, is Paul thinking
of a one-off prayer in an emergency. His language implies a regular habit.
But it implies more: the confidence that, whether our specific prayers are
answered or not, our lives are held "in Christ", and so are our loved ones,
whether they know it or not, even whether they believe it or not. So, at a
deeper level than our specific requests, we can trust that "all things shall
be well, and all manner of things shall be well" (Mother Julian).

But Mother Julian's words must not obscure the many *cris de coeur*
offered to God in the Bible. There are many prayers of petition in Old
and New Testament alike which are more like cries of desperation or
despair than prayers. In St Mark's version of the stilling of the storm,
for example (Mark 4:35–41), Jesus answers his disciples' desperate plea
for help, even though he recognizes that they have no faith (verse 40).
(In Matthew's and Luke's versions they are not much better—Matthew

---

5   Markus Bockmuehl, *The Epistle to the Philippians* (London: A & C Black
     Ltd., 1997, 4th edition), p. 24.

8:23–7; Luke 8:22–5.) St Paul' prayers, too, would sometimes have been very like those of Jeremiah or Job—an anguished cry or even an angry shout in a crisis. Even if a nervous breakdown or depression was not behind the despair he describes in 2 Corinthians 1:8, Paul does not try to hide from the Corinthians how he felt:

> We were so utterly, unbearably crushed that we despaired of life itself.

It is difficult to be sure what had happened to Paul. Whatever it was, he goes on to write confidently of "God who raises the dead" (verse 9) and of how

> He who rescued us from so deadly a peril will continue to rescue us . . .
>
> *Verse 10*

The ups and downs of Paul's life and ministry are clear. But we should not miss the hope and resilience which shines through again and again:

> I have learned to be content with whatever I have . . . I can do all things through him who strengthens me.
>
> *Philippians 4:11b–13*

and

> May the God of hope fill you with all joy and peace in believing . . .
>
> *Romans 15:13*

But perhaps the most instructive of all Paul's references to prayer, explicit or implicit, is when he writes of his "thorn in the flesh" (2 Corinthians 12:7b–10). We can't be sure what the "thorn" was: epilepsy or a debilitating skin complaint have been suggested. But it was an ailment serious enough to make the Corinthians wonder whether, as one scholar once put it, "a sick apostle was a contradiction in terms".

Whatever it was, Paul uses language reminiscent of the book of Job: it was "a messenger of Satan". But also, "*it was given* to me"—as if God had a hand in this affliction in allowing it at all. There is a parallel in Jesus' own life when, at the outset of his ministry, the devil (Satan) tempted him in the wilderness, but it was the Holy Spirit who "drove" (Mark's language) or "led" (Matthew and Luke's word) him there.

Paul's prayer for healing seems not to have been answered at all at first. "Three times I appealed to the Lord about this . . . " (2 Corinthians 12:8). Eventually, Paul seems to imply, the answer came:

> My grace is sufficient for you, for power is made perfect in weakness.
>
> *Verse 9*

Here, I suggest, is the New Testament's "bottom line" in petitionary prayer. It is implied in "Give us today our daily bread"—not necessarily what we want, but what we need. That distinction, of course, isn't easily made. We don't always know our needs, especially our deepest needs, and sometimes we think that what we want is what we need.

The central image for us here is "father"—not a masculine image, but rather an image of love and care. The God and Father of our Lord Jesus Christ is utterly different from the unjust judge who eventually and reluctantly accedes to the persistent demands of the widow in Jesus' parable (Luke 18:1–8):

> . . . your heavenly Father knows that you need all these things . . .
> do not worry about tomorrow . . .
>
> *Matthew 6:32,34; even imperfect human beings know*
> *how to give good gifts to their children, cf. Luke 11:13*

Jesus' own experience in Gethsemane takes us deeper still. He prayed desperately for deliverance from a cruel death ("Take this cup from me"), but such a deliverance did not come. As we saw in the previous section, two of our Gospels, Mark and Matthew, suggest that at the very end Jesus felt utterly God-forsaken. The resurrection transformed the disciples' perception of the cross: God had been there after all—in the person of Jesus himself.

Prayers of asking are not always answered in the way we hope. But what *is* always given is a mysterious, life-giving grace which is the hallmark of God's own presence. We may not know it at the time, but Old and New Testaments are unanimous: it will never fail us. That is the Bible's "bottom line" in asking.

Ask "in my name"—and persevere

As often, John's Gospel and the first letter bearing his name seem to have the last word. For example, "God is love" (1 John 4:8,16) is the best place to begin in the Bible if we want to unravel all that it says about God. Similarly, the first verse of John's Gospel, ("In the beginning was the Word . . . and the Word was God") makes explicit what the other Gospels imply about Jesus. And so with the teaching of Jesus about prayer: "Ask and you will receive" becomes "Ask *in my name* . . . ". Three times in the last discourses in John, Jesus promises

> If you ask anything *in my name I will do it.*
> *John 14:14; 15:16; 16:23*

We recall that a name in the Bible was much more than a name. It denoted a person's character and purpose: all that that person was about. To pray in Jesus' name is to pray as Jesus prayed, and though Christian wisdom—and surely the Lord himself—encourages us to pray as we can, this is the goal: to want what Jesus wanted—the hallowing of God's name, the coming of his kingdom, the doing of his will. As the Psalmist quoted earlier (Psalm 37:4) promises, if, above all, we want God himself, God is more than ready to give unreservedly to us his very life and glory (John 17:3,22–3).

The God and Father of Jesus is the very opposite of the unjust judge of the parable of Jesus, as we noted earlier in this chapter. God

> ... does not ignore the orphan's supplication, nor the widow's ...
>
> *Ecclesiasticus 35:14*

Nor is God reluctant to give, as another parable in Luke's Gospel makes clear (11:9–13; cf. 6:35,38). Yet Jesus emphasizes perseverance in prayer, especially in Luke's Gospel (see also 21:36). The early Church taught and practised the same: "Persevere!" (Romans 12:12; 1 Thessalonians 5:17; Acts 2:42). Jesus' teaching implicitly picks up what we have found in the Psalms: God sometimes seems slow to respond, and it's easy to lose heart.

A final thought. We forget that, Son though Jesus was (John 1:18; 3:16), he is also "first-born of many brothers and sisters" (Romans 8:29; Hebrews 2:10–12). We are not "second-class" sons and daughters, as Jesus' prayer in John's Gospel shows:

> The glory that you have given me I have given them, so that they may be one, as we are one.
>
> *John 17:22*

In the light of this, some words of St Paul seem to be the appropriate conclusion for our exploration of "asking God":

> If God is for us, who is against us? He who did not withhold his own Son, but gave him up for all of us, will he not with him also give us everything else?
>
> *Romans 8:31b,32*

Conclusion

Biblical prayers of asking are gritty, realistic, and often confident. Both Old and New Testaments encourage those who pray to "cry out to the Lord"—tell God what is on your heart—persevere, and trust. The Bible is also realistic in recognizing that bad things happen to good and bad people alike. "The prayer of the righteous is powerful and effective", says the letter of James (5:16). But neither Job in the Old Testament nor Jesus in the New were spared acute suffering.

Yet Jesus introduced a deeper note of trust and confidence in "the heavenly Father" who "knows what you need before you ask" (Matthew 6:8). "Ask and you will receive." But this didn't and doesn't exempt followers of Jesus from life's many ups and downs. Paul had to live with his "thorn in the flesh", whatever it was, but with the assurance that God's grace would suffice; God's power is "made perfect in weakness" (2 Corinthians 12:9).

What John's Gospel adds to the teaching of Jesus in the other Gospels—"Ask *in my name*"—is crucial here. We are to pray as Jesus prayed. The Lord's Prayer is the norm. The golden rule seems to be: "Tell God what is on your heart; he knows what you need." *And learn to want God above all else:* "seek first the kingdom ..." and the God revealed supremely in the cross and resurrection of Jesus will give you the desire of your heart (Matthew 6:33; Psalm 37:4).

Prayer

Eternal God, your Son Jesus taught us to call you Father. Help us to believe that you know what we need before we even ask. Teach us to trust you in life and in death, give us day by day our daily bread, and help us to want you in all things and above all things.

For reflection and discussion

1. Reflect on your prayers of "asking": what do they say about you and your priorities?
2. "Ask God for the big things, and the little things will take care of themselves" (Clement of Alexandria). Do you find this helpful advice?
3. Share experiences of "unanswered" prayers. How did such experiences affect your faith?

8

Standing before God for others

Then Jesus said, "Father, forgive them; for they do not know
what they are doing."

Luke 23:34

It is Christ Jesus who died, yes, who was raised, who is at the right
hand of God, who . . . intercedes for us.

Romans 8:34

If our asking God for things in prayer is sometimes uncertain and
confused, so too are our prayers for others. Is it presumptuous to pray
for other people—an infringement of their free will? For whom should
we pray? How does intercession—praying for others—work?

The quotations which introduce this chapter focus on the Bible's
supreme intercessor, namely Jesus. The outstretched arms of Jesus on
the cross lift all humanity to God: "Christ on the cross lays one hand on
God's shoulder and the other hand on each human shoulder."[1] The cross
is the heart of the Christian understanding and practice of intercessory
prayer—*standing before God for and with others.*

In this chapter, we look in turn at standing before God for others
in the Old Testament and in the New, before exploring the practice of
praying for others today.

---

[1]   Enzo Bianchi, *Words of Spirituality* (London: SPCK, 2002), p. 61.

Abraham's barter with God and other Old Testament prayers

Many people in the Bible stand before God on behalf of others. Abraham's prayer for the people of Sodom and Gomorrah is the first of many.

The conversation between Abraham and God (in Genesis 18:22–33) is one of the most extraordinary in the entire Bible. God has noted the wickedness of the two cities of Sodom and Gomorrah, and their destruction is clearly imminent. There follows an exercise in bartering. I paraphrase and summarize, even though a bald summary cannot hope to convey the entertaining, lively detail of the original.

> Abraham: Suppose there are only 50 righteous people in Sodom? Will you destroy them too?
>> God: No. If there are only 50, I will not.
>> Abraham: Suppose there are five short of that 50 . . . ?
>> God: No—I still won't destroy the city.
>> And so it went on.
>> Abraham: Suppose only 30 . . . 20 . . . 10 . . . ?
>> God: For the sake of 10 I will not destroy it.
>
> *Verse 32*

This Abraham story will be difficult for most of us today. (Whether this is in any way historical is not the point.)[2] It seems to imply that, unless someone intercedes for wrongdoers, God will punish them. We should not jump to conclusions. The golden rule of Christian interpretation of the Bible is: *interpret in the light of Jesus.* An incident from the Gospels is relevant here. James and John wanted to call down fire from heaven on a Samaritan village which would not welcome Jesus and his disciples. But Jesus "turned and rebuked them" (Luke 9:55). A later Christian scribe elaborates that terse statement: Jesus went on to say, "You do not know what spirit you are of, for the Son of Man has not come to destroy the

---

2   On the difficult subject of violence attributed to God in the Bible, see my *Who on Earth is God?* (London: Bloomsbury, 2014), Chapters 1 and 2.

lives of human beings, but to save them" (verses 55b and 56).[3] In other words, "Elijah might have done that, but it is not my way."

The Old Testament offers more iconic examples of intercession. Moses prays desperately for the people of Israel when they turned from God to worship a golden calf:

> Alas, this people has sinned a great sin . . . But now, if you will only forgive their sin—but if not, blot me out of the book you have written.
>
> *Exodus 32:31–2*

This is not the only time when Moses will intercede for the people. Even here, despite Israel's failure, all is not lost; their journey towards the land God has promised them continues—and so do Moses' prayers for them (Exodus 33:13; 34:9).

As with the Abraham story, a Christian reader of this story will interpret it in the light of Jesus, recalling the Jesus who offered his life "a ransom for many" (Mark 10:45). St Paul, as a follower of Jesus, once expressed himself in a way similar to the prayer of Moses in Exodus:

> I could wish that I myself were accursed and cut off from Christ for the sake of my own people . . .
>
> *Romans 9:3*

There are many more examples in the Old Testament of individuals standing before God in prayer for the people of Israel. Later in their history Isaiah stood with them: "a man of unclean lips . . . among a people of unclean lips" (Isaiah 6:5). King Hezekiah is portrayed as a man of prayer, praying for the deliverance of Judah from King Sennacherib of Assyria (2 Kings 19:15–19) and for the healing of the ritually unclean amongst the people (2 Chronicles 30:18–19).

The leaders of Israel stand before God for the people because that is their vocation. They take personal responsibility for their faithlessness. Ezra, "appalled" at the inter-marriage of many Israelites with the resident

---

[3]   Luke 9:55 and 56a are usually printed as a footnote in modern translations.

population of Canaan (Ezra 9:1–4),[4] prayed for them: "I am humiliated, my God . . . I am ashamed my God to lift my face to you. Our sins tower above, and our guilt is so great that it reaches to high heaven" (9:6).

Ezra's prayer is a long one (9:6–15), the people repent, and God's anger is averted (10:12–14).

We shall need to ask later whether "averting" God's anger is compatible with our understanding of a Christlike God. For now, we note again the complete solidarity of the intercessor, Ezra, with the people for whom he prays.

Daniel's prayer (Daniel 9:4–19) reads like the work of the writer of the book which bears Daniel's name. But that is not the point. It is another example of a national leader praying with and for his people:

> While I was speaking and was praying and confessing my sin *and the sin of my people Israel* . . .
>
> *Verse 20*

As with Moses, Isaiah and Ezra, there is no distinction between the one who prays and the people for whom he prays. But, once more, we find a difficult reference to God's wrath:

> O Lord, in view of all your righteous acts, let your anger and wrath, we pray, turn away from your city Jerusalem, your holy mountain . . .
>
> *Verse 16*

The background to the prayer is made clear in an earlier verse: the devastation of Jerusalem and its Temple by the armies of Babylon in 587 BCE.

Does there ever come a time when an intercessor simply gives up on the people for whom they pray? It is not a theoretical question. Jeremiah, it seems, came close to giving up:

---

[4]   It would be unwise to draw contemporary lessons from that prohibition (if such it was) of inter-marriage. In the crisis Ezra faced, the very survival and identity of the nation of Israel were at stake.

> The Lord said to me: Even if Moses and Samuel stood before me,
> I would not be moved to pity this people
>
> *Jeremiah 15:1*

Perhaps Christians suffering today under a government which seems irredeemably evil will pray, not for its conversion but for deliverance from it. On the other hand, a parent praying for a child who has gone off the rails is unlikely ever to give up. So, to adapt an argument of Jesus (Luke 11:13), "how much more" will God persevere with even the most recalcitrant of his children! *The cross of Jesus, and Jesus' eternal intercession "at God's right hand", surely mean that God never gives up on anyone.*

Old Testament examples of intercession show that great spiritual resources are required of the one who intercedes. Telling God what is on our heart—praying as we can—is one thing; a prayer of costly empathy is quite another. "The bind . . . is that what most people need to overcome their selfishness is a life of prayer, but their very selfishness prevents them from being able to pray."[5]

As well as prayers for the nation, there are prayers for individuals in the Old Testament, too many for us to note in full here. David, for example, prays for Bathsheba's sick child, though the child dies nevertheless (2 Samuel 12:16,18). Benaiah prays for Solomon, the new king (1 Kings 1:36–37), Elijah for the widow's dead son (1 Kings 17:17–23), and Elisha and Gehazi, his servant, for the dead boy of another woman (2 Kings 4:33). In both these cases, both boys are raised back to life.

One more intercession concerns us here because of its urgent contemporary relevance for us:

> Pray for the peace of Jerusalem.
>
> *Psalm 122:6*

For Christians today, this prayer needs a wider context than it has in the Old Testament. The coming of Jesus resulted in a change of focus

---

[5]   Shai Held, *Abraham Joshua Heschel: The Call of Transcendence* (Bloomington, IN: Indiana University Press, 2013), p. 203.

amongst his disciples (though not, perhaps, immediately, as the disciples continued to pray in the Temple in Jerusalem). But many of them, especially Gentile Christians, came to regard Jesus himself as the Temple (e.g. John 2:13–22), not the building in Jerusalem. That revolution in their understanding of God reshaped their prayers. So today Christians will continue to pray, not just for the peace of Jerusalem, but for the well-being of both Israelis and Palestinians, and the peace of the whole world.

Patriarchs and prophets, then, prayed for Israel. But our leading quotations at the beginning of this chapter suggest that the intercessions of the Old Testament foreshadow the intercession of Jesus himself. As often, the New Testament "lies hidden" in the Old (St Augustine). But, as we turn to the New Testament, we shall need to return to the difficult concepts of God's punishments and God's wrath. Does prayer somehow avert them?

The crucified Jesus

The crucified Jesus for Christians is the role model for intercession, so fulfilling the intercessions of the Old Testament. That fulfilment means, in practice, the extension of the light and truth of God to the whole world. So that also means that the intercession of Jesus, through the resurrection, is now revealed as universal and eternal (Romans 8:34; 1 John 2:1–2). For this reason, there can be no limit to the scope of Christian intercessions, as a later letter in the New Testament makes clear:[6]

> First of all, then, I urge that supplications, prayers, intercessions, and thanksgivings be made for *everyone,* for kings and all who are in high positions, so that we may lead a quiet and peaceable life . . .
>
> *1 Timothy 2:1–2*

A summary follows of the foundation for that ministry of intercession:

---

[6] Most scholars are inclined to attribute the letters to Timothy and Titus to a later interpreter or disciple of Paul.

> For there is one God;
>
> there is also one mediator between God and humankind,
>
> Christ Jesus, himself human,
>
> Who gave himself a ransom for all.

Verses 5–6

This seems an image too mysterious or difficult to grasp: God standing before God with and for the whole world. God the Son offers his eternal prayer—his life and death—for the world's healing and wellbeing. It does not mean that the Son of God pleads our cause before a Father otherwise bent on our punishment. Nor does it mean the Son enabled the Father to forgive by undergoing our punishment in our place. There is no division in the Godhead: God is love (1 John 4:8 and 16). All that God—Father, Son and Holy Spirit—does for the life and wellbeing of the world is the work of love from start to finish.

Both the love and the "wrath" of God are in both Old and New Testaments. Yet the words "wrath" or "anger" (Greek *orge*), when used of God can be misleading. The symbol of darkness best represents what God's "wrath" means; it is God "hiding his face" (e.g. Isaiah 64:7) at human sinfulness. This symbol of darkness will help us understand what the cross of Jesus means, as we explore the mystery of Jesus' intercession for us and for the whole world.

The first three Gospels portray the hour of Jesus' death as *simultaneously* the revelation of God's love and God's wrath. This is what the three hours of darkness over the whole earth symbolizes (Mark 15:33; Matthew 27:45; Luke 23:44). Never before had there been a revelation like this of the cost and sacrifice of divine love, *and* never before had there been such darkness: a revelation of how far humankind has distanced itself from the Creator.

The loving father in the parable of the prodigal son is fundamental to the Christian understanding of God. Yet the cross of Jesus adds even deeper meaning to the parable. The cross represents, as Karl Barth suggested, the mission of God's Son into the far country of human darkness and sin (Chapter 6). The cross marks the ultimate reach of God's search for the prodigal, *and* our distance from God "in the far country".

This is why Christians have regarded the cross as an "at-one-ment"—
the reconciliation of the creation with its Creator: Jesus holding together
in his own person both God and the world. Language about "averting"
God's wrath (as in the Old Testament) can be misleading. "Satisfying"
God's wrath, a later expression in Christian tradition, is similarly
misleading. Rather, the cross *reveals* God's "wrath"—God's "withdrawal",
creating a darkness in which humankind loses its way. Yet even in the
heart of the darkness, love has the last word—as the resurrection reveals.
"The light shines in the darkness, and the darkness did not overcome
it" (John 1:5). In the language of our theme in this chapter, Jesus, Son of
God, prays eternally for us and all the world.

In the light of this, how are we to pray for others? We recall, first,
how important forgiving others is in the teaching of Jesus. A parable
contrasts our forgiving with God's (Matthew 18:23–35): a king forgives
his servant the equivalent of 15 years' wages (verse 24) and that same
servant refuses to forgive a fellow-servant 100 days' wages (verse 28). But
our relationships with God and with other people are inseparable, as the
Lord's Prayer indicates. (On this see also Chapter 5.) Any failure in love
is bound to affect adversely our prayers.

The sharpest challenge of all is how disciples of Jesus respond to their
"enemies"—as Jesus himself made clear:

> But I say to you, Love your enemies and pray for those who
> persecute you.
>
> *Matthew 5:44*

Luke's Gospel has a similar verse:

> Bless those who curse you, pray for those who abuse you.
>
> *Luke 6:28; cf. Romans 12:14; 1 Corinthians 4:12*

Enzo Bianchi argues that loving our enemies is "a summary of the gospel".
He goes on to quote the early Christian writer Tertullian: "All people love
their friends, but only Christians love their enemies." Such love requires
a costly spiritual journey involving the discovery that we ourselves are
"enemies", loved by God and for whom Christ died. "An enemy" is our

greatest teacher, because he or she unveils what is in our heart. But what is in our heart doesn't emerge when we're on good terms with others.[7] Really praying (that is, from the heart) for our "enemy" becomes a searching experience; the more pressure we are under from other people, the harder it can be not only to pray for them, but also *what* to pray.

"Enemies" in this context of prayer is a word which also includes all the people about whom we complain and grumble—everyone, in fact, about whom we are inclined to harbour negative thoughts. Praying for them all has a crucial place in Christian spirituality. Otherwise, we're pretending—being "nice" perhaps, but hardly honest before God.

We turn next to St Paul, whose remarks on this subject take us to the heart of the gospel and of prayer.

A church leader in the 1990s remarked that the biggest theological change of the twentieth century was the growing Christian belief that God himself suffers. (The First World War was a potent influence here.) Paul's intercessions for his churches, like the prayers of Moses and the prophets for Israel, reflect that divine suffering. Sharing the pain of God comes to expression most powerfully in the letters to Corinth, especially 2 Corinthians. Death and life, sorrow and joy belong together in Paul's graphic self-portrait:

> . . . always carrying in the body the death of Jesus, so that the life of Jesus may also be made visible in our bodies . . . So death is at work in us, but life in you.
>
> *2 Corinthians 4:10 and 12*

Passages like this one (cf. 1 Corinthians 4:9–13; 2 Corinthians 6:2–10) have been rightly described as the heart of Paul's understanding of the God who—he had come to see—bears the pain and sin of the whole world. It is this understanding of God which is the basis of Paul's own ministry of intercession, and of the Church's vocation to be a "kingdom of priests" (Exodus 19:6; 1 Peter 2:9).

Paul's own prayers for his churches are examples of this costly intercession. His earliest letter, 1 Thessalonians, is typical. Paul both

---

7   Bianchi, *Words of Spirituality*, pp. 92–3.

gives thanks and prays for his churches (1:2). The prayers, like the thanksgivings, are the tip of the iceberg: Paul was *always* giving thanks and praying for his churches. The cost and pain come through:

> ... we were gentle among you, like a nurse tenderly caring for her own children.
> ... when, for a short time, we were made orphans by being separated from you ...
>
> *1 Thessalonians 2:7,17*

This is remarkable language from a man in a patriarchal, male-dominated world. Another letter confirms this picture. Paul describes himself as " ... a minister of Christ Jesus to the Gentiles in the priestly service of the gospel of God, so that the offering of the Gentiles may be acceptable ... " (Romans 15:16).

Intercessions, like thanksgivings, are frequent in the New Testament letters—especially those of Paul. They are expressed in greetings, such as "Grace to you and peace from God our Father and the Lord Jesus Christ" (e.g. 1 Corinthians 1:3) and in "prayer-wishes" (as scholars have called them):

> May the God of hope fill you with all joy and peace in believing, so that you may abound in hope by the power of the Holy Spirit.
>
> *Romans 15:13; cf. verse 5; 1 Thessalonians*
> *3:11–13; 5:23–4, amongst several others*

Behind them all is the experience which is the foundation of both Christian living and intercession:

> The grace of the Lord Jesus Christ, the love of God, and the communion of the Holy Spirit be with all of you.
>
> *2 Corinthians 13:13*

Perhaps it is not possible for the weekly intercessions of a Christian congregation each Sunday to reflect the pain and anguish of many of the Bible's intercessions. It is more than most of us can sustain. And yet, if the New Testament is to be our canon—our "measuring-rod"—sharing the pain of God is an inescapable part of Christian living and praying. Indeed, countless unsung churches across the world live this experience day after day, week after week. (More of this in the next section.)

In this costly ministry of praying with Jesus in Gethsemane, as Dietrich Bonhoeffer described it, followers of Jesus have a special responsibility to pray for each other.[8] There are many "each other" commands in the New Testament letters—so many, in fact, that only a sample can be given here.

I begin with the command which Paul calls, quite simply, "the law of Christ":

> Bear one another's burdens . . .
>
> *Galatians 6:2*

The word "load" (Greek *bare*) implies a weight too great to bear alone— as the preceding verse implies; such loads, carried alone, are likely to tip people into sins such as despair. Paul then goes on to say that each must carry their own load (Greek *phortion*, verse 5), he is thinking of the pack of the individual soldier; it's his, and his alone. In this context, we might say that the Christian's "pack" will always include costly prayers of intercession.

There are many more "each other" commands: "bear with one another . . ." (Colossians 3:13; compare Ephesians 4:2); "encourage one another . . ." (1 Thessalonians 4:18; 5:11); "beloved, do not grumble against one another" (James 5:9; cf. 4:11), and, most frequent of all, "love one another", as in "love one another deeply from the heart" (1 Peter 1:22).[9] The phrase "from the heart" shows that this is a world away from just being nice to each other: keeping up appearances in a public place, and quietly grumbling away in private.

---

[8]   D. Bonhoeffer, *Letters and Papers from Prison* (London: SCM Press, 1967), p. 125.

[9]   Other commandments to love each other in the New Testament include Romans 12:10; Galatians 5:13; 1 Thessalonians 3:12; Hebrews 10:24 and 1 John 3:11.

More "each other" commands show that the behaviour required here also requires a far-reaching transformation of hearts and minds:

> Let us . . . no longer pass judgement on one another.
>
> *Romans 14:13*

Most extraordinary of all, perhaps, is this:

> Do nothing from selfish ambition or conceit, but *in humility regard others as better than yourselves.*
>
> *Philippians 2:3*

And the relevance of prayer to all this? Surely what Jesus said about his disciples' failure to heal someone applies here too:

> This kind [i.e. an unclean spirit] can come out only through prayer.
>
> *Mark 9:29*

> Therefore confess your sins to one another and pray for one another so that you may be healed.
>
> *James 5:16*

Confessing *to one another* seems like a huge spiritual challenge. But should it be? "Keeping up appearances" is not what Church and Christian faith are about.

Praying for other people today: Where the Church often goes wrong

If the cross—the outcome of our Creator God living our life and dying our death—is the icon of Christian intercession, it puts a question-mark against a widespread misunderstanding:

> The content in much intercessory prayer divides sharply into
> those who pray and those who are prayed for ... There is lack of
> both humanity and Christianity whenever we take up an attitude
> of the fortunate pitying the unfortunate and praying for them.
> What is needed are, not prayers which divide, but prayers which
> "uncover *the fundamental unity of all* ... "[10]

We don't just pray *for* others, but *alongside* them. We can't pray well, for
example, for people over whom we stand in judgement. Intercessory
prayer will often require a new "heart" for those for whom we pray—
people of other faiths, terrorists, people in prison, the politicians we love
to hate ... "Judge not ... " (Matthew 7:1), however, doesn't mean "Stop
making moral judgements" about, for example, oppressive economic
policies. It *does* mean we shouldn't write people off or demonize them—
including the authors and agents of such policies.

Jeremiah was a prophet who felt the pain of God more than most. His
advice to the Jewish exiles in pagan Babylon is remarkable:

> Seek the welfare of the city where I have sent you into exile, and
> pray to the Lord on its behalf, for in its welfare you will find
> your welfare.
>
> *Jeremiah 29:7*

A superior stance of judgement and semi-detachment from "the world" is
not open to disciples of Jesus. Our baptism into Christ, "the last Adam",
means we have well and truly joined the human race—as God did in
the incarnation. Our standing before God with and for others will be a
deeply human ministry of prayer.

A final question—and one often asked about prayers for others—is:
"How does intercession work?" Here, I think, we need to set aside the
language of God "intervening". The word "intervene" is misleading. It
suggests that God is outside the situation we're praying for, and has to
step in to answer our prayers. But God is already there—present, always

---

[10]   R. E. C. Browne, *Love of the World: Meditations*, ed. Canon Ian Corbett
       (Worthing: Churchman Publishing, 1986), pp. 136–7, my italics.

and everywhere, in every situation. The Bible is insistent about that. But the God who is love is, by that very definition, a *non-coercive* God. We mislead ourselves by more misleading language—of God being "all-powerful" and "in control". God's power and "control" have to be understood in the light of the cross (1 Corinthians 1:18–25).

God's way of working is a covenantal one: God commits himself to work with us—with our faith, love, hope and prayers. Our prayers for others, offered in the Spirit of Jesus, are used by God to create "pathways of grace"—i.e. God's grace. That grace will evoke, in the situation we pray for, all the natural and human potential *which is already there*, but seldom realized because of our human limitations.

Sometimes a "miracle" does indeed happen. A healing, for example, exceeds entirely all the potential, natural and human, of the situation prayed for. When that happens, we can recall with gratitude to God "the power *which is at work among us* to do immeasurably more than all we can ask or conceive . . . " (Ephesians 3:20–1).[11]

Prayer

God and Father of us all, we dare to ask that we may pray as Jesus prayed. May we stand with others not in judgement, but in love. Deliver us from our prejudices, hatreds, and unkind thoughts, that we may pray for them in the Spirit of your Son. Make us the truly human family you meant us to be.

---

[11] The final paragraphs of this section owe much to the helpful discussion about intercession in *The Faith of a Christian* by J. A. Baker (London: Darton, Longman & Todd, 1996), pp. 159–62.

For reflection and discussion

1. Take time to explore the ways in which the Old and New Testaments are similar, and the ways in which they differ on the theme of "standing before God for others". Why is the cross of Jesus so important?
2. How can we help each other to avoid making intercessions routine and shallow?
3. How can we "stand before God" with and for people of whom we thoroughly disapprove, without the "us" and "them" of uncharitable judgements?

9

Profile of love: Praying the Psalms

Then I said, "Here I am . . . I delight to do your will, O my God;
your law is within my heart."

Psalm 40:7a,8; Hebrews 10:7

There is none like you among the gods, O Lord, nor are there
any works like yours.

Psalm 86:8

Why are the Psalms so neglected today? Church congregations and
individual Christians read and pray them less often. Selections in
contemporary hymnbooks illustrate the problem. We understandably
want to exclude vengeful-sounding references to "enemies", but this often
means excluding other features of the Psalms, such as questions and
protests about life, the state of the world and God. Leaving out psalms
which refer to "enemies" also has the unfortunate effect of leaving out
most of the references in the Psalms to "the poor", since the "enemies"
(whoever they were) oppressed the poor.

Much contemporary worship expects us to "look on the bright side
of God" (as someone once put it); better a happy chorus than a pre-
Christian lament from the Psalms. Yet, as a great Old Testament scholar
wrote, if the twentieth-century churches hadn't so neglected the Old
Testament, we should have coped far better than we have done with
contemporary atheism. As it is, we pay a heavy price for our neglect of
the Psalms in narrowed horizons and diminished theologies.

Using the Psalms isn't easy. But they are part of the *canon* (literally,
"measuring-rod") of Scripture. How do our prayers measure up to them?
It's been said that no one believes, prays, praises and protests like the

Psalmists. (On praise in the Psalms, see also Chapter 10.) The Psalms are whole-hearted, full-blooded and earthed in reality. Dietrich Bonhoeffer, the Lutheran pastor who died at the hands of the Nazis at the end of the Second World War, believed that by using the Psalms regularly we will "grow into" them.

That has been my own experience. Some Psalms I still find difficult, even impossible to pray, and I'll return to the question of how "unchristian" some of the Psalms seem to be in their cries for "vengeance" and in their portrayals of God's anger.

In this chapter we shall look at

- Jesus and Christian faith in relation to the Psalms—including "enemies"
- the strange, God-centred world of the Psalms
- the potential of the Psalms to be a prayer book "for all seasons".

Finding Jesus, ourselves—and "enemies"

From the very beginning Christians believed that the Psalms were fulfilled in the life, death and resurrection of Jesus (e.g. Luke 24:44; Romans 15:3). Not only did Jesus utter the words of a psalm in his last hours (Mark 15:34; Luke 23:46), the early Church also found his profile in the Psalms. The unknown "righteous sufferer" of the Psalms (as he is sometimes called) is identified with Jesus, as in Paul's quotation from the Psalms:

> The insults of those who insult you have fallen on me.
>
> *Romans 15.3; cf. Psalm 69:9*

The early church also identified "the king" ("Son of David") in the Psalms with Jesus—as the writer to the Hebrews does more than once, quoting Psalms 2, 45, 102 and 110—all in one chapter! (See Hebrews 1:5,8,10–13.)

The "profile" of Jesus the Christ appears, too, in the Psalms' frequent references to the law (that is, the law of Moses, traditionally, the first five books of the Old Testament). Bonhoeffer came to value greatly the psalm which might seem to us interminable: Psalm 119, with its 176 verses, and its repeated references to the law. A Benedictine friend of mine finds it helpful—as I do—sometimes to substitute the name "Jesus" or "Christ" for "law" (and other related words) as he reads that psalm. After all, Paul taught that "Christ was the fulfilment (*telos*) of the law" (Romans 10:4). Similarly, when Psalm 19 moves seamlessly from a consideration of "the heavens" to "the law of the Lord", a Christian reader might recall the New Testament's teaching of how all things were created in, through and for Christ (e.g. Colossians 1:15–20).

From St Paul onwards, Christians have believed that Jesus was "the ultimate human being" (literally, "the last Adam", 1 Corinthians 15:45). In the Psalms our conversation with God comes to its clearest and fullest expression. As we grow into the Psalms, we begin to find our voice—a voice we didn't know we had—the voice of Jesus. What the Psalms can do and will do if we let them is to draw out of us cries and aspirations we didn't know were there:

> O God, you are my God; eagerly I seek you.
>
> *Psalm 63:1*

> "Come", my heart says, "seek his face!"
> Your face, Lord, do I seek.
>
> *Psalm 27:8[1]*

Together, Jesus and the Psalms form the heart and centre of the Bible's prayers, and in his story—above all, his relationship with the One he called "Father"—we find our true story. As a well-known hymn has it, Jesus is the "Heart of my own heart".

But what of the many psalms, or sections of psalms, which seem sub-Christian? "Enemies" in the Psalms are variously described: for example, they are arrogant, proud and oppress the poor. The Psalmist's enemies

---

[1] Rowan Williams in his book *On Augustine* (London: Bloomsbury, 2016) has some helpful things to say about the Psalms, and the "profile" of Jesus in them.

are the enemies of God. How are we to use these psalms, if at all, in our prayers?

A word of explanation about the language may help. The Psalmists had *stock images* on which to draw. Enemies are described as a hostile army (3:1; 27:3 etc.), hunters and fishers (e.g. 7:15; 31:4 etc.), and wild beasts such as lions and dogs (7:2; 22:12–13; 59:14 etc.). The same images keep occurring, and so do the same themes, such as the conviction that the wicked will fall into a net of their own making/ their evil "will recoil on their own heads", (7:16—similarly 9:15–16; 10:2; 57:6 and others).

Other words in the Psalms are easily misunderstood. "Vengeance" doesn't mean hatred and revenge, but putting right what is wrong when normal processes of justice have failed. Hence the prayer to the "God of vengeance" (Psalm 94) in the context of the oppression of the poor reflects the conviction that God will exercise justice. The eager anticipation of the "God who comes to judge the earth" (Psalm 98:9) has the same meaning: the God who will put right what is wrong.

To return to the "enemies", who these were we can't now say, and perhaps that is just as well. We can't straightforwardly equate their lack of belief in God with atheism today. The "ungodly" of the Psalms are deceitful and unjust, and the poor and needy are their victims. That can hardly be said of all atheists today. I have known people who considered themselves atheists but who regularly attended church and were more Christlike than some who professed to believe in God.

The voice of the Psalmists in these conflicted situations still needs to be heard. The Revised Common Lectionary, widely used around the world, reflects a pattern similar to contemporary hymnbooks, and, as we noted earlier, a reduced focus on "enemies" means a reduced focus on their victims—the poor. (The lack of attention to poorer nations by the richer ones illustrates the biblical picture only too well.) The challenge for Christians today is to take these psalms seriously without demonizing rich people. Our "fight", as one New Testament letter puts it, isn't against human beings, but against " ... cosmic powers ... " (Ephesians 6:12). Those words are a healthy caution against identifying "the enemy" too readily with people we disapprove of. The Psalter's fierce condemnations of enemies have to be read in the light of the command of Jesus: "Love your enemies" (Luke 6:27–9,35; Matthew 5:43–8).

Many Christians today say their prayers only too conscious of "enemies on all sides"—Christians in Iraq, Pakistan, northern Nigeria and elsewhere. We can read the Psalms in solidarity with them. They, like us, seek to pray the Psalms with Jesus and in the spirit of Jesus.

In this spirit, we shouldn't overlook the crucible of acute suffering out of which some of the Psalms came. The experience of ancient Israel was very different from the experience of most of us in the comfortable West. The tiny nations of Israel and Judah were at the mercy of powerful empires to the south and east—Egypt, Assyria, Babylon. Even in their own lands, many of them would have suffered at the hands of unscrupulous, ruthless kings. What they lived through, including the destruction of Jerusalem and its Temple in 587 BCE, is reflected in some of the Psalms (see, for example, Psalm 74:1–11). Against this background, the shocking prayer-wish about the children of Babylon becomes more understandable:

> Happy they shall be who take your little ones
> And dash them against the rock!
>
> *Psalm 137:9*

As one scholar has remarked, Psalm 137 is "an honest expression of real emotions in the presence of God . . . In the immediate wake of Babylon's cruelty to them forgiveness would have been phoney; their anger . . . has the virtue of being real."[2] It helps to explain, too, those Psalms which celebrate God's past victories over the enemies of Israel (e.g. Psalms 66:6–7; 78:42–55; 105:26–38; 135:8–12; 136:10–24).

It takes time to grow into the Psalms and make them our own as far as we can. In doing so, we remember that the Psalms were the prayers of Jesus, and that love was central to his life and teaching, and, consequently, central to Christian faith.

There is a further question for the Christian reader of the Psalms to face. The theme of God's victory over evil and evildoers resounds through the Psalms:

---

[2]   Anthony de Mello SJ, *Sadhana, a Way to God* (Anand, India: Gujarat Sahitya Prakash Anand Press, 1980), p. 45.

... though the wicked sprout like grass
And all evildoers flourish,
They are doomed to destruction forever,
But you, O Lord, are on high forever.

Psalm 92:7–8; cf. 94:23; 145:20

That seems to sit uncomfortably with much of the New Testament, not to mention our own aspirations for reconciliation and peace in the world today. It is crucial to interpret these verses, too, in the light of our faith in a Christ-like God. According to Paul, humankind has made itself an "enemy" of God. *But God has not responded in kind*:

God proves his love for us in that while we were still sinners Christ died for us . . . If, while we were enemies, we were reconciled . . . , much more surely . . . will we be saved by his life.

Romans 5:8–10

The abolition of enmity between humans and God bears fruit also in peace between peoples previously estranged or hostile, such as "Jews" and "Gentiles" (Ephesians 2:14–16).

The New Testament, like the Old, looks to a final triumph over enemies:

For he [Christ] must reign until he has put all his enemies under his feet.

1 Corinthians 15:25, echoing Psalm 110:1

"The last enemy" here is death (v. 26). So perhaps God's "enemies" in the end are the human race's enemies, particularly those idols which make their worshippers less than human (Psalm 115). In our day ideologies such as a rapacious capitalism, or a fierce nationalism, often function as "gods"—that is, the ultimate reference points by which our lives are governed. By contrast, the real God is on the side of life and of human beings—all of them.

With this in mind, we return to the Jesus in whom the Psalms were realized and fulfilled. Jesus is the Son spoken of in Psalm 2:7. He is the sufferer *par excellence* (see especially Psalms 22:6,18; 69:8,21). He is also the one who receives the life and joy which God has promised to the sufferer who is faithful:

> I keep the Lord always before me;
> Because he is at my right hand, I shall not be moved . . .
> For you do not give me up to Sheol,
> Or let your faithful one see the Pit.
> You show me the path of life . . .
> *Psalm 16:8–11a; quoted in Acts 2:25–28a*

All of this helps to show what New Testament writers mean in their conviction that Jesus "fulfilled" the Psalms: he realized their fullness— both promise and potential. His Spirit has helped Christians to pray them ever since.

The strange God-centred universe of the Psalms

There is still more for us in the Psalms in their vision of a God-centred universe.

We live in an age which is human-centred in all kinds of ways. "Man is the measure of all things", and such a human-centred outlook shapes religion, too—particularly in the so-called developed world. Whilst the people of the Bible ignored secondary causes—a point I return to—"our modern view of reality is equally, and more grossly, partial, for it seems to ignore the Primary Cause entirely".[3]

In our day, one consequence of this human-centred outlook is that prayer can be diverted into DIY spirituality, and contemplation confused with transcendental meditation or mindfulness. The Church, too, becomes church-centred instead of God-centred—often, in the process, becoming secularized in its outlook and its management, with models borrowed uncritically from other professions or from business. A deeper

---

[3] S. Terrien, *The Psalms: Strophic Structure and Theological Commentary* (Grand Rapids, MI: Eerdmans, 2003), p. 652 (commenting on Psalm 92).

immersion in the God-centred world of the Psalms will assist our prayers, worship and mission.

The God-centred character of the Psalms is clear from start to finish. But God is not where our prayers usually begin. The problem is our preoccupation with ourselves and our own concerns. We have our "shopping lists" for God—especially requests for ourselves, our churches and people we naturally care about. God does not despise our shopping lists, and making "our requests known to God" is often necessary if God is to free us from anxiety (Philippians 4:6). We may have to start where we are, not where we would like to be. But the Psalms encourage us to go deeper.

The God-centred world of the Psalmists was dominated by the "unfailing love" and "wonderful deeds" of the Lord. The love and the deeds go together; they form the Psalmists' entire horizon. There is no better image of the Lord's unfailing love than the sky:

> Lord, your unfailing love reaches to the heavens,
> Your faithfulness to the skies.
>
> *Psalm 36:5*

It stretches, it would seem, into infinity. Stand outside and look up, and the sky is everywhere. Where does it end? You can't tell. It appears to be bounded by the horizon, but it is not. Or, instead of looking into space, think of time; God transcends this boundary, too. God's love endures *for ever*, and that is because

> From everlasting to everlasting you are God.
>
> *Psalm 90:2*

This divine *environment* of ours—the everlasting God whose love reaches to the skies—is also an infinitely intimate companion. The Psalmist talks to God almost as an equal, but in a way which doesn't diminish God's holiness—i.e. God's complete integrity in relating to us and his world.

The Psalms have many images for God: king, shepherd, rock, shield, judge, tower, fortress, stronghold, shelter, help, saviour, redeemer . . . The One to whom we pray is far more than these images; they are more like windows on to what God is and does. The image of a rock, for example, suggests God can't be got round, and is the surest possible foundation for our life; the Rock permits "no fissure, no deviation, no detour".[4]

There are other images, constituting what has been called "the anatomy of a personal God", such as God's eyes, ears, hand, mouth, voice, and face. There are verbs to match, as in the picture given in Psalm 53:

> God looks down from heaven on humankind
> to see if there are any who are wise,
> who seek after God.
>
> *Verse 2*

It's been well said that these days we find difficult all this poetic imagery for God because we live in an age which, with its increasingly functional, targeted educational programmes, tends to neglect literature and poetry. Regarding the Psalms as poetry does not mean they are fiction or theological fantasy. Poetry often gets to the heart of things where prose does not. Definitions and accurate descriptions of the mystery which is God are impossible. That is why we use approximate language: images, metaphors, analogies. With such religious poetry, we "read the text as a lover reads, with a tensile attentiveness that wishes to linger, to prolong, to savor . . .".[5]

Other prominent words in the Psalms about God can enrich our prayers. "Righteousness" is a difficult but important word. (It is, perhaps rightly, retained in the more literal translations of the Psalms.) It means God's consistency in judging and "saving"—that is, not only putting right what is wrong, but also acting in the interests of our deepest human wellbeing—individuals, nations and the whole world.[6] The fact that God is architect, guardian and redeemer of the world's moral order gives urgency and focus to our prayers: "Your kingdom come, your will be

---

4   William P. Brown, *Seeing the Psalms: A Theology of Metaphor* (Louisville, KY: Westminster John Knox Press, 2002), p. 13.

5   See my book *Who on Earth is God?* (London: Bloomsbury, 2014), pp. 105–7.

6   Sister Margaret Magdalen CSMV, *Jesus: Man of Prayer* (London: Hodder & Stoughton, 1987).

done . . . " includes the vision of a God who rescues the poor, thwarting the plans of their oppressors (Psalms 9:18; 12:5; 14:6 etc.).

It is far from obvious to most of us in the so-called "developed" world that this is a God-centred universe, created, pervaded and ruled by the One whom the Old Testament calls *Yahweh*, "the Lord". The Psalmist insists God "sits enthroned for ever" (Psalm 9:7; cf. 11:4; 29:10 etc.). It is not easy to go on trusting that a fundamentally non-coercive God "reigns". But the challenge of the Psalms is inescapable: do we really believe its picture of a God-centred universe—and live as if we do? David Watson, a saintly Anglican, at the height of the troubles in Northern Ireland, led a large congregation in one of Dublin's cathedrals in shouting "The Lord reigns."

The very different worldview of the people of the Bible has to be recognized. They seem to ignore what we might call secondary causation, whereas, for them, God, the "Primary Cause" does everything. Isaiah offers one of the clearest examples:

> I am the Lord, and there is no other.
> I form light and create darkness,
> I make weal and create woe;
> I the Lord do all these things.

Isaiah 45:6c,7

The Psalmist does the same:

> He [God] makes wars cease . . .

Psalm 46:9

> [God] gives food to the hungry.
> The Lord sets the prisoners free . . .

Psalm 146:7

Does God really do these things? The state of the world may suggest otherwise. But these words need to be taken seriously. God *is* at work, principally in human minds and hearts; where else will a non-coercive

God work, except in seeking to win hearts and minds? It takes two—God and humankind—to make the kind of world purposed by Love.

A prayer book for all seasons

In Chapter 1, we noted that today's world is busier, faster, noisier. Against this background of today's hectic schedules, the Psalms are an invaluable resource. It is a prayer book for all seasons; to coin a phrase from church liturgies, prayers for "always and everywhere", as the Psalms themselves illustrate.

Mornings are a good time to be reminded of, and to declare God's "steadfast love", just as night time is the time to proclaim his "faithfulness" (Psalms 92:2; 143:8). There need be no time of day untouched by prayer: "before dawn" (Psalm 119:147), "at all times" (Psalm 34:1), at bedtime (Psalm 4:8), "in the watches of the night" (Psalms 63:6; 119:148).

Other psalms take a longer view. Psalm 71 is the prayer of someone who, now old, can look back on a life of prayer:

> For you, O Lord, are my hope,
> my trust, O Lord, from my youth . . .
> So even to old age and grey hairs,
> O God, do not forsake me . . .
>
> *Verses 5 and 18a*

The panorama of prayer in the Psalms extends everywhere. No situation is beyond the reach of God. There is no place too far for him to reach; light and darkness make no difference to God:

> The Lord my God lights up my darkness.
>
> *Psalm 18:28b; cf. 139:7–12*

No crisis is too dire or hopeless for prayer: "out of the depths" (Psalm 130:1) is a phrase appropriate for many psalms, including the psalm which, according to the Gospels of Matthew and Mark, was on the lips of the dying Jesus:

> My God, my God, why have you forsaken me?
>
> *Psalm 22:1; Mark 15:34; Matthew 27:46*

There are many more such laments in the Psalms (Psalms 38, 55, 74, 77 and 88 are examples). Lament has become, as one Old Testament scholar puts it, "a lost art" in a church culture which tends to filter out negative emotions such as anger, distress and despair—and, sometimes, honesty in our relationships. We also tend to exclude anger, distress and despair from our pictures of Jesus. But here in the Psalms is the whole of human life, as it is in the Bible as a whole. Here, especially, Christians have heard the voice of Jesus and recognized the contours of his life and death.

So, in the Psalms, "the prayer of humanity comes before God ... *Someone, somewhere* is feeling angry or hurt, full of revenge or full of wonder, needy and despised, exalted and blessed ... ".[7] Even Psalms which read mostly like a rant teeter on the edge of prayer: "the Psalter shows that even barely grappling with what is going on in our lives is actually some sort of prayerfulness".[8]

Despair, like anger, is not easily accommodated in the spiritual life. But it is frequently expressed, as when God seems far away:

> O Lord, why do you cast me off?
>
> Why do you hide your face from me?
>
> *Psalm 88:14*

The silence or absence of God "does not drive Israel away from prayer; it drives Israel to more earnest, intense, passionate prayer—to the very You who will not answer".[9]

In this prayer book for all seasons, the Psalmist is never less than whole-heartedly engaged. The "heart"—centre and soul of our being—is

---

[7]   Margaret M. Daly-Denton, *Psalm-Shaped Prayerfulness. A Guide to the Christian Reception of the Psalms* (Collegeville, MN: Liturgical Press, 2011), p. 98.

[8]   W. Brueggemann, *The Psalms and the Life of Faith* (Minneapolis, MN: Fortress Press, 1995), p. 56.

[9]   Brueggemann, *The Psalms and the Life of Faith*, p. 56.

mentioned often in the Psalms (e.g. Psalm 27:8; cf. 63:1), and "hearts" need some attention, as the Psalmists well knew. What is needed is "an undivided heart" (Psalm 86:11); hence the prayer, "God, create a pure heart for me . . . " (Psalm 51:10). Such purity requires time—time for God. So waiting—waiting for God—becomes important:

> For God alone my soul waits in silence.
>
> *Psalm 62:1a*

In sum, the Psalms are a prayer book for all seasons not only because they reflect a discipline of constant prayer, but also because of their worldview: they make a world (in the process, unmaking false worlds), the centre of which is God. They are a prayer book for Christians as well as for the Israel from whom they came because disciples of Jesus see in him the fulfilment and transformation of Israel's prayers and praises.

Deciding where a chapter on the Psalms should be in this book was not straightforward. But I think it belongs here—in the response to Jesus. The place of the Psalms in the worship and prayers of the Church since the coming of Jesus suggests as much. The Psalter is the profile of the Love "which endures for ever", the Love revealed in Jesus. It is meant to be prayed. But, to echo Bonhoeffer once more, it takes time to grow into this.

Prayer

God, you are my God. Unlike our substitute gods, you are God always and forever. In your unfailing love and righteousness put right all that is wrong in my life and the life of the world. So may the world's poorest people receive the justice you want for them, and those who wish them harm be turned from their evil ways.

For reflection and discussion

1. Reflect on the pressures, priorities, habits etc. which marginalize God in personal life, church life, and the life of the wider world. How may the Psalms help us?

2. Read together a psalm which refers to "enemies" and share the difficulties in making it a Christian prayer.

3. If praise, like faith, is something "caught, not taught", how may we/a church "catch" the spirit of praise? What do the Psalms suggest?

1 0

Praise: The enjoyment of God

Let everything that breathes praise the Lord!
Praise the Lord!

Psalm 150:6

I have said these things to you so that my joy may be in you and
that your joy may be complete.

John 15:11

Why are Christians, when praising God, not always a very appealing
sight? In Chapter 8, I suggested that Christian intercession doesn't
distinguish between "us" and "them"; it "uncovers the fundamental
unity of all". That must be so, if we pray in the spirit of the Son of God
who identified himself fully with humankind. Does this apply also to
Christians at praise? There are other fundamental questions to be faced
about praising God. In this chapter, we shall ask

- Is the God of both Old and New Testaments *praiseworthy*?
- Do the praises of the Bible reflect a *subversive* God?
- Are we supposed to *enjoy* God? Is that the secret of the Bible's
  praises—and of evangelism? Will Christians truly praising God
  attract others?

Is the God of both Old and New
Testaments praiseworthy?

The question has to be asked. A few years ago, I discovered that many Christians accept unquestioningly the stories in the Bible in which violence is attributed to God. We disguise the violence a little by talking, for example, about "the Exodus", rather than "the Plagues of Egypt and God's massacre of the Egyptians' firstborn". Or we refer to "Israel's Conquest of Canaan", instead of "God's Annihilation of the Canaanites".[1] There is violence attributed to God in the New Testament, too—especially if we include the book of Revelation.[2] Is the God of the Bible really worthy of praise?

Two crucial observations will help us here. First, one verse is a vital clue to the whole Bible: "God is love" (1 John 4:8,16). That doesn't mean we can forget the rest. But everything else has to be understood in the light of that. The second key point is this: the purpose of the Bible is to help us to love God with all our hearts and our neighbour as ourselves—the two great commandments (e.g. Mark 12:28–34). If we are really to praise God, we need to learn how to love God, and even to enjoy God. In the words of the Psalm already quoted in this book, "Delight in the Lord" (Psalm 37:4). But to do these things, we shall need God's help.

With this in mind we return, first, to the Psalms. Their Hebrew name is *Book of Praises*. That suggests that all its contents, even the laments, are one great chorus of praise. The five books which make up the Psalter all end with doxologies (Psalms 41:13; 72:18–19; 89:52; 106:48; 150:6). These praises express Israel's response to what God has done—the "deeds" and the "works" of the Lord. All of them are signs of God's dependability—his "steadfast love", "faithfulness" and "righteousness". They include the world's creation (e.g. Psalm 104), Israel's creation (e.g. Psalm 100:3), and "my" creation (Psalm 139:13–16). They include also

---

[1] See my *Who on Earth is God?* (London: Bloomsbury, 2014), pp. 49–53.

[2] *Who on Earth is God?*, pp. 223–7. Yet John reserves much of his most severe language, not for human beings, but for supernatural evil—including, in his view, its contemporary embodiment, the Roman Empire.

the many times God rescues from trouble both the one who prays and the people of Israel.

This brings us to an important feature of God's praise in the Bible. *Humans are not required to abase themselves when they praise God.* Contrast what happens when we are ordered to praise a dictator. God—unlike most human rulers—is not so remote or exalted that he fails to notice even the lowliest person. In the Bible, two themes often go together: God's majesty *and* God's intimate friendship with the poor and humble:

> The Lord is high above all nations,
> and his glory above the heavens . . .
> He raises the poor from the dust,
> and lifts the needy from the ash heap . . .
>
> *Psalm 113:4–7*

Even more remarkable, *the glory of God and of human beings go together.* Irenaeus, second-century bishop of Lyons, wrote of how the glory of God is "a human being fully alive". A psalm says something very similar:

> O Lord, our Sovereign,
> how majestic is your name in all the earth!
> What are human beings that you are mindful of them,
> mortals that you care for them?
> Yet you have made them a little lower than God,
> And crowned them with glory and honour.
>
> *Psalm 8:1,4,5*

The praise of the living God, unlike the praise of false gods, exalts humankind as well as God. Other gods are, literally, life-less, and a danger to life, especially human life:

> They have neither knowledge nor understanding,
> they walk around in darkness;
> all the foundations of the earth are shaken.
>
> *Psalm 82:5; cf. 115:3–8*

In the New Testament, the pattern is the same. The exaltation of Jesus means our exaltation too. God shares his glory with us (John 17:22; Romans 8:21,29–30). The pivotal figure is "the Son of Man", Jesus' preferred way of referring to himself. The letter to the Hebrews links Psalm 8, which we have just noted, with Jesus, son of man (Hebrews 2:6–9).

The secret of Christian praise lies in discovering, however gradually, that God is unreservedly "for us". The gift of Jesus, God's own image and ultimate word to us all, means that the God "who did not withhold his own Son . . . will . . . with him also give us everything else" (Romans 8:32). It may take a lifetime to make this wonderful discovery. Others come to it through one life-changing conversion. But all of us need to discover it again and again if our praise of God is to be genuine.

For many people today, however, the question of whether God is worthy of praise depends on whether there is a "place", traditionally called "hell", to which God sends people who don't believe in him. The Bible may seem to say this, and many Christians believe it. I am not so sure. Even if there are a few verses which point that way, are they the dominant voice? Mustn't they be interpreted in the light of our master text, God is love?

True, there are fierce warnings and images of divine judgement and separation both in the Old and New Testaments, and we mustn't gloss over them with bland statements about everyone "getting to heaven in the end". A full discussion of this is impossible here. But two points need to be made. First, even the often-fearsome book of Revelation is more open than might first appear. At the end, the book of life is not closed but remains open (22:10). The erstwhile opponents of God, "the kings of the earth", finally enter the holy city (21:24; contrast 18:3 and 19:19)—the city where the leaves of the trees of life are "for the healing of the nations" (22:2). There are fierce exclusion clauses (e.g. 21:27 and 22:15), but that brings me to a second point. Given the Bible's rock-like conviction that the love of the Lord "endures forever", we may well wonder—as the Psalmist does—whether that love ceases even at death (Psalm 16:10–11, quoted by Peter on the day of Pentecost (Acts 2:25–8)).

Is everyone destined (pre-destined?) to enjoy the glory and praise of God? No one is frogmarched into praise. Compulsory praise is a contradiction in terms. But the universal scope of God's purpose in the Bible is unmistakable. God wants everyone to be saved (1 Timothy 2:4), and the Bible's conclusion in Revelation envisages God making his home "among mortals". This NRSV translation, however, doesn't do justice to the original Greek which refers to "humankind" (*ton anthropon*—plural).

Even before the end, there is a widening circle of praise in the Bible, Israel and the Church playing pivotal roles. It is Israel, through the Psalmists and the prophets, who first issues the invitation to "the nations". True, there are psalms where the nations are "the fall guys" in the story of God's care of Israel (e.g. Psalm 105:26–36,44). But other psalms have a much more universal view. Psalm 67 is one such psalm:

> May God be gracious to us and bless us
> and make his face to shine upon us,
> that your way may be known upon earth,
> your saving power among all nations.
> Let the peoples praise you, O God!
>
> *Verses 1–3a*

Prophecies too (e.g. Isaiah 2:2–4; 25:6–7) envisage the universal praise of God, to which the whole of creation lends its voice—as it always has, long before humankind came on the scene (e.g. Psalms 19 and 104). Praise is the vocation of the whole world, and, ultimately, its joy. So every living person is invited to join the chorus of praise. Five psalms of praise, all beginning and ending with *hallelu-yah* conclude the book of Psalms. "Here there are no urgent questions—no 'Why?'s or 'How long?'s ... There remain only 'Songs of Praise' which put everything else in perspective."[3]

The Bible's answer to our question is "Yes—God is supremely praiseworthy", and God's faithfulness and love are the fundamental reason why. But before we return to our theme of the enjoyment of God, there is another striking feature of the Bible's praises that we must see.

---

[3]   R. Davidson, *The Vitality of Worship: A Commentary on the Book of Psalms* (Grand Rapids, MI: Eerdmans, 1998), p. 469.

The Bible's subversive praises

None of us can make ourselves praise God. Praise—to be genuine—has
to be spontaneous. Compulsory or spurious praise is a lie, and demeans
us. The praise of God, by contrast, is our glory too. In the Bible it is also
often *subversive*—our theme in this section.

An early example is the Song of Moses in the book of Exodus (15:1–
18). Echoes of that song reverberate throughout the Bible:

> I will sing to the Lord, for he has triumphed gloriously . . .
>
> *Verse 1a*

> Who is like you, O Lord, among the gods?
>
> *Verse 11a*

The Song of Moses celebrates the drowning of Pharaoh and the Egyptian
army in the Red Sea. Taken literally, this is a difficult subject to include in
the praise of God. But, as we have seen with other Old Testament stories,
we are a long way from history here. Yet the story and the folk memory
of God's *subverting power* was iconic. That power was real, and it shaped
a whole people and their religion.

The Old Testament's subversive praises continue. The Song of
Hannah, mother of Samuel, anticipates the Song of Mary (1 Samuel
2:1–10; Luke 1:46–55) in its reversal of roles of strong and weak, rich
and poor. Many psalms keep asking whether any gods are comparable
to "the Lord"—the living God (e.g. Psalms 71:19; 86:8). Idols—impostor
gods—usually serve vested interests. This is why praising the "living" God
in the Bible—a thumbing of the nose at the idol—is subversive.

God's challenge to false gods is always—as in the Psalms—the
beginning of God's rescue of the oppressed and the poor. Old and New
Testaments are united on this theme. But as we move into the New
Testament, the identity of "the enemy" changes. In Exodus, it is the
pursuing Egyptians; in the New Testament "the enemy" is no longer
other nations, but the forces of evil and oppression. There is no place for
demonizing anyone; there are, ultimately, no human enemies (Ephesians
6:12). The book of Revelation is a partial exception, since the writer

sees the Roman Empire and its rulers as evil. But even here the greatest
enemy is a supernatural evil, symbolized by the "beast" of Chapter 13
and onwards.

Against this background the Bible ends as it began:

> The Lord will reign for ever and ever.
>
> *Cf. Exodus 15:18 and Revelation 11:15*

Three songs of praise in Luke's Gospel are subversive in the way they
envisage a world turned upside down. The Songs of Mary, Zechariah and
Simeon (Luke 1:46–55; 1:67–79 and 2:29–32) are full of Old Testament
echoes. As we have seen, the Song of Mary echoes the Song of Hannah;
the Songs of Zechariah and of Simeon are mosaics of images and phrases
from the Psalms and the prophets.

The Songs of Zechariah and of Simeon also herald a new dawn.
References to "enemies" still occur (1:71 and 74), but the horizon is
transformed; other nations are not the enemy anymore. Instead, there
now shines "a light for revelation to the Gentiles . . . " (2:32). No longer
are there any outsiders, foreigners or people "outside the gate" because
God in the person of his Son has been there (Hebrews 13:12–13), and
so relativized all barriers and boundaries.

In Luke's Gospel, people are always praising God. But most often
it is the poor: shepherds, for example (2:13–14,20), and, as well as the
poor, "the captives . . . the blind . . . and the oppressed", mentioned in
Jesus' "manifesto" at Nazareth and his reply to John the Baptist (4:18
and 7:22–3) and later healed by him (e.g. 5:25; 13:13; 17:15; 18:43).
The crowds who witness those healings also praise God (e.g. 5:26). In
this Gospel's final scene, the disciples "were continually in the temple
blessing God" (24:53).

The other Gospels strike different notes, yet glorifying God remains
the backcloth to what Jesus is doing. "The mountain", place of revelation
in Matthew, is the setting of a climactic healing scene (15:29–31). Jesus
heals the lame, the maimed, the blind, the mute and many others, and
huge crowds praise "the God of Israel". In Mark's Gospel, praises are less
prominent. The response of the crowd to Jesus' healing of the paralyzed
man is an exception (Mark 2:12), but here, too, praise is subversive;

God is "glorified" whatever "the scribes"—the biblical authorities of the day—might think (verses 6–8).

In John's Gospel, the picture changes, and so does the language. The theme will be the divine glory (1:14). The wedding at Cana anticipates the revelation of that glory (John 2:1–11), since the story epitomizes Jesus' life's work, transforming the "water" of human life into the "wine" of God's abundant life (John 10:10). But here, too, the overall effect is subversive. The supreme moment of glory is the crucifixion, as the prayer of Jesus shows:

> Father, the hour has come; glorify your Son so that the Son may glorify you.
>
> *John 17:1*

A more subversive icon of praise than a crucified man could hardly be imagined.

In the New Testament, as in the Old, praises rise to God through and beyond the darkness. As we saw in the psalms of lament in the last chapter, praise is often offered to God against a threatening background. In the Gospels, the coming of the Light activated forces of darkness. The crowds' "Hosannas" in Jerusalem quickly faded (e.g. Mark 11:1–11), but in the gathering darkness, Jesus and the disciples in the upper room still sing their praises to God—probably the final Hallel, Psalms 115–118 (Matthew 26:30; Mark 14:26).

The pattern of the Old Testament is repeated in the New: God's people praise God through setbacks, persecution and hardship, subverting hierarchies of wealth and power, and challenging accepted values and norms. It happens still, as I discovered during a visit to the Christians of Sierra Leone shortly after the civil war there. Praise to God, then and now, is offered in the face of, or in spite of, the powers that be.

The biblical background to praise, and the praises of many in extreme circumstances today poses searching questions for us. Can we be too comfortable really to praise God? We rightly thank God "for all the blessings of this life" (as in the Church's General Thanksgiving), and Christian wisdom has always insisted that we should not go looking for suffering and martyrdom. Yet the testimony of the Bible is well-nigh unanimous: those who have known the depths of life praise God best. The psalms uttered by the dying Jesus are not only laments but also psalms of praise (Mark 15:34; Matthew 27:46; Luke 23:46).

The cross, then, is the very heart of the Bible's subversive praises. Jesus, crucified and risen, is worshipped as "Lord" and "Son of God". Both these titles were claimed by, and attributed to, Roman emperors. The book of Revelation, with its image of a "slaughtered Lamb"—i.e. the crucified Jesus—sharing the very throne of God (e.g. Revelation 5:6–14), was a powerful riposte to Roman imperial propaganda.

The "doxologies" (literally, praises which give glory to God) of Revelation—are among many which occur in the New Testament. Doxologies often take the long view. Some look back:

> Now to God who is able to strengthen you ... according to the mystery that was kept secret for long ages but is now disclosed ... to the only wise God be the glory through Jesus Christ forever. Amen.
>
> *Romans 16:25–7*

The letter to the Hebrews refers to the "eternal covenant", but looks also to the immediate past, in its reference to

> the God of peace, who brought back from the dead our Lord Jesus, the great shepherd of the sheep ...
>
> *Hebrews 13:20*

Another New Testament doxology looks forward:

> Now to him who is able to keep you from falling, and to make you stand without blemish in the presence of his glory with rejoicing, to the only God our Saviour, through Jesus Christ our Lord, be glory ... before all time and now and for ever. Amen.
>
> *Jude 24–5*

Whilst the Bible does not teach techniques of praise (what would they be anyway?), it can help tired, demoralized congregations to recover their vocation of praise—provided we face the challenge of the Bible's subversive praise: against idols and the vested interests they represent the living God takes the side of the oppressed and the poor. This, too, has a rightful place in the Church's and the world's joyful celebration of God.

The re-discovery of praise and evangelism today

God's grace and love, revealed supremely in the cross and resurrection of Jesus, create not just songs, but lives of praise. The whole of life is lived "to the glory of God": eating, drinking—everything (1 Corinthians 10:31). A church's hard-won unity, involving acceptance of Christians very different from ourselves, is to the glory of God (Romans 15:7). Christ-centred, sacrificial living "multiplies" human thanksgivings "to the glory of God" (2 Corinthians 4:15). Even something as contested as Paul's collection for poverty-stricken Jewish Christians will culminate in the praise of God (2 Corinthians 9:12–15). In all of this, praise "lifts up" not only God, but also the human beings whose lives are praising God.

With this in mind, we return to our leading theme, the praise and enjoyment of God.

C. S. Lewis, in his early days as a Christian, found the whole idea of praising God difficult. Why, he wondered, should God "want to gratify his appetite" in this way? "I don't want my dog to bark approval of my books." But then he began to see the close connection in human life between praise and *enjoyment*: " . . . *enjoyment spontaneously overflows into praise*". This is why "the world rings with praise"; human life teems with examples. What is more, "praise not merely expresses but completes the enjoyment", as when two people in love voice their adoration and love for each other. "The delight is incomplete till it is expressed." So enjoying and praising God belong inseparably together.[4]

This understanding of praise can transform the mission and evangelism of the Church. Stephen Sykes notes the negative image which has dogged Christian evangelism since the nineteenth century, and goes on:

---

[4]   C. S. Lewis, *Reflections on the Psalms* (London: Geoffrey Bles, 1958), quotations from pp. 90, 93 and 94.

The proposal I wish to make is that the praise of God, in word and deed, should be the leading context and motive for evangelising. The urgency of evangelism stems from Christians longing to share the sense of gratitude which overwhelms them, in the light of God's gracious gift of himself. They should make no distinction between insiders and outsiders, between, as it were, the probably saved and the possibly damned.

Sykes points out that often, in evangelism, what Christians communicate is their own anxiety and "a certain desire to dominate. Instead, it is as if Christians were extending an invitation to join a choir to someone known to have a good voice . . . The invitation is extended to all . . . It is based on gratitude for what God has already done, and a longing that God's praises will grow."[5]

We can put this important point in another way. A Christian enjoying being a Christian is a good advertisement for her faith. But the enjoyment has to be unselfconscious. And it has to be far deeper than a church congregation simply enjoying its own company. The heart of the matter is the enjoyment of God, as the Westminster Confession has it: "the end of man [sic] is to love God and enjoy him forever."

Conclusion: Praise in the end

In Revelation, the Bible's last book, the song of Moses is joined to that of "the Lamb", the crucified and risen Jesus. It is the grand finale of a great symphony:

Great and amazing are your deeds,
Lord God the Almighty!
Just and true are your ways . . .
For you alone are holy.
All nations will come

---

[5]   Stephen Sykes, *The Story of Atonement* (London: Darton, Longman & Todd, 1997), pp. 152–3.

And worship before you,
For your judgements have been revealed.

Revelation 15:3–4

Despite all the doubtful interpretations of it, the Book of Revelation concludes our Bible for a reason: *praise in the end* in the presence of our Creator who from the beginning has called humankind to find our life, our unity and our joy in his friendship. Praise is offered to God *and to the Lamb*. "God and the Lamb constantly appear side by side in Revelation, which means that human beings are constantly in God's heart."[6] The incarnate, crucified and risen Christ is the secret of the hope-filled, triumphant praises of God in the New Testament, including Revelation. The image of the Lamb upon the very throne of God also precludes any kind of Christian "superiority complex" or triumphalism.

This book, like most of the Bible, testifies to God's unwavering commitment to putting right what is wrong in his world. The end, of course, is not yet, as the author of Revelation well knows. It ends with one final prayer and blessing (Revelation 22:20–1).

In the vocation of praise to which all are called, countless people have gone before us. The book of Revelation tells us that they are already singing in heaven. Their praises seem to invite all creation to join in:

Then I heard every creature in heaven and on earth . . . singing,
"To the one seated on the throne and to the Lamb
be blessing and honour and glory and might
for ever and ever!"

Revelation 5:13

The Church today needs this hinterland of heaven to inspire and deepen our praises.

---

6   Christina Le Moignan, *Following the Lamb* (Peterborough: Epworth Press, 2000), p. 29.

Prayer

O God, why can we not praise you? Forgive us that we are so deaf to you, our life and our joy. Forgive us that we are often deaf to your unflagging call of love. Awaken and warm our hearts, make radiant our lives and our faces that we may praise you as you deserve, and draw others to the warmth of your love.

For reflection and discussion

1. Why do so many Christians and churches find it hard to praise God—as opposed to "going through the motions"?
2. Are suffering and hope—perhaps two sides of the same coin—the secret of the praises of the New Testament?
3. In the light of the Bible's testimony about "delighting in the Lord" (Psalm 37:4) and C. S. Lewis' remarks quoted in this chapter, whatever happened to our *enjoyment* of God?

1 1

Love answering love: Summary and conclusion

God is love, and those who abide in love abide in God, and God abides in them.

1 John 4:16b

Abide in me as I abide in you. Just as the branch cannot bear fruit by itself unless it abides in the vine, neither can you unless you abide in me.

John 15:4

(Another) imaginary letter from God

Dearly Beloved,

Yes, still "beloved", through everything, in spite of everything. It seems we have travelled a long way together in the short time since my coming amongst you. My world has changed almost out of all recognition. Love—my love—although it was present before, has taken deeper root amongst you. Its message has spread.

And yet, beloved as you will always be, you are still far off. You have mistakenly imagined me as too much like yourselves; you think my freedom is a threat to yours when, in truth, it is the key to yours; you think my sovereignty is a threat to yours, when, in truth, I have invited you to share mine. The earth, too, though mine, I have gladly entrusted to you—and it grows weary through your restlessness.

You still have not found your true rest—your true love. You are right to reject all the false images of me, but still you court substitute gods, not heeding a gathering darkness and a fragmenting world. Do not, I pray, reject me, for you and I belong together. Why? That is the mystery of Love—the mystery of my being: "I will be what I will be."

It's time to come home—not to an immaturity I never wanted to imprison you within, nor to "heaven" as you used to imagine it, but to "a new heaven and a new earth" where hunger and tears will be no more. Come home to your true Centre, and find the joy and love for which I made you.

Praying through the Bible—a summary

Although human beings have always prayed to "whatever gods there be" as far back as our evidence takes us, the biblical story begins with God. In the beginning was God's own prayer: God's call of love to us all. It is a universal call. The stories of Adam and Eve, made in God's image, and of God's invitation to Abraham and Israel into partnership ("covenant"), become our human story. God's call to us is not narrowly religious. It is the call of "Wisdom", a call to discover life as God intended it to be. The New Testament fulfils the Old Testament: God's love revealed in Jesus and given to us through the Spirit enables us to pray and to begin to live that life (Chapter 3).

It takes two to make a conversation, and God's call to us all invites our response. For each of us, it's an invitation to discover "the real me and the real God" (C. S. Lewis). In the Bible's all-too-human responses to God's call there is no lack of doubts, questions and protests. All these responses are a kind of praying, because beginning to get real before God is to pray. The ideal, iconic response to God is that of Mary: "Here am I . . . let it be with me according to your word" (Luke 1:38).

The only real God of which the Bible speaks (the "living" God) is present always and everywhere, though that is often far from apparent. This God is a God of surprises, present when least expected, sometimes apparently absent when desperately wanted, and yet, whatever it feels like, a God who is always near and who hears prayer (Chapter 4).

Prayer, according to Jesus, is opening our hearts to "the Father" and putting God first (God's name, God's kingdom, God's will). Because we pray "*Our* Father", it is a prayer we say with and for potentially everyone. It is a prayer which commits us to trusting God for what we need each day, and letting go ("forgiving") all that other people have said or done to our detriment, so that God's forgiving love may reach our hearts. We commit ourselves, too, to God to deliver us from our failures and from the power of evil.

The Lord's Prayer is a prayer to say and to live each day. Such a prayer doesn't come naturally to disciples—as the Gospels show. What matters is that Christ prays within us, as we move from being "semi-detached disciples" to disciples "in Christ". Our prayers become rooted in the eternal prayer of Jesus in God's own heart (Chapter 5).

This brings us to what a great theologian called the happiness of prayer. Thankfulness is at the heart of Christian living and praying, as the letters of the New Testament show. The centre of worship for Christians from earliest days has been *the* Eucharist (*the* Thanksgiving). Its remembrance of the betrayal, crucifixion and resurrection of Jesus, testifies to God's invincible, redeeming love at the heart of all things.

"Confessing" belongs here because God's unconditional grace gives us the faith and courage to face who and what we are, as the parable of the prodigal son shows (Luke 15:11–32). Confession becomes a gift: in the presence of Love we can accept ourselves and come home. What we can't or won't do, God, who "works through our freedom without undermining it" (James Alison), makes possible (Chapter 6).

Prayers of asking in the Bible are often blunt and direct, characterized both by "crying" in anguish and a deep though challenged confidence in God. Old and New Testaments alike, (Elijah, Job, Paul—and Jesus) show that God doesn't always answer our prayers when or in the way we hope. John's Gospel "glosses" the teaching on prayer in the other Gospels: ask *in my name* and you will receive. "The name" of Jesus is not a password, like a pin number, ensuring our prayers "get through". Rather, we pray in the spirit and character of Jesus, sharing his purpose. Such growing into Christ will refine and simplify what we want to ask God for. Wanting and seeking God in all and above all is the road, and the promise: God will give you "the desire of your heart" (Psalm 37:4).

The Old Testament gives us many examples of people praying for others. But the supreme icon of intercession is Jesus, arms outstretched on the cross and in heaven "at the right hand of God". Praying "in Christ" deepens and widens our prayers for other people. The disciples of Jesus came to see there was no limit to the people for whom they should pray (1 Timothy 2:1). Jesus had urged them to pray for their "persecutors" (Matthew 5:44; Luke 6:28). By extension, that includes anyone hostile or even critical towards us—and, of course, people towards whom we feel the same. There can be no "us" and "them" in prayers offered in the name of Jesus (Chapter 8).

The Psalms hold a special place. They are the prayers of Israel, but from the beginning the Church recognized in them both the profile and the prayers of Jesus. Christians read them, grow into them and pray them in the light of Jesus. The soaring heights and the depths of their prayers, their human grittiness, the light and the darkness portrayed in them—even (false) gods and "enemies"—all make the Psalms a "prayer book for all seasons", revealing to us prayers and praises which we did not know we had in us (Chapter 9).

Misunderstandings about prayer extend into praise. Real praise, even under a dictator, can't be done to order. Nor can our praises of God. But the God revealed in the Bible is truly praiseworthy. Its climax and heart are found near the end: "God is love" (1 John 4:8,16). In the Bible, it is God who evokes praise—for his "works" in creation, the Exodus, and, most of all, the cross and resurrection of Jesus. Such praise doesn't demean us. Rather, God sharing with us God's very being and life ("glory"), is the foundation of our humanness and our praise, in which all creation joins and to which all are invited. This enjoyment of God in praise can be an attractive, effective way of evangelizing.

The Bible's praises are often subversive, because the real God works to subvert the world's oppressive powers, exacting sacrifices from the needy and the poor. In the Gospels and in the Psalms, especially, people praise God's care of oppressed and marginalized people. The heart of praise in Revelation, the Bible's last book, is the Lamb with the marks of suffering, representing our place at the very throne of heaven. The context of praise in the end is "a new heaven and a new earth" when God's presence and glory will evoke continual praise (Chapter 10).

In the next section we shall seek to apply these findings to the twin challenges with which we began in Chapters 1 and 2: praying and reading the Bible. But first, a preliminary observation which applies to both. The world we are part of tends to have a very functionalist view of things: what are they *for*? How are they *relevant*? Such a view can taint, and even corrupt our view of the most holy things—including human beings. We humans, like the worship of God, friendship and marriage—and the Bible—are *more than relevant*. We demean these holy things when we talk about their relevance.

We need a less functionalist view of both reading the Bible and praying. We are not looking primarily for answers, results, or even relevance. In both activities we are seeking, above all else, simply *to be* in God's presence, to enjoy his love, and to grow towards deeper prayer and the love and compassion which are its surest outcomes.

Reading the Bible well and praying from the heart

We began, in Chapters 1 and 2, by recognizing that praying and reading the Bible are challenging and problematic for many people today. The Bible has many obscure, difficult passages. In our churches it may be heard but seldom understood. Preachers find it hard to explain or interpret difficult passages to their congregations. The busyness of our modern way of life makes it even harder to practise the time-honoured Christian disciplines of daily prayer and Bible reading. In this section, I shall try to draw some practical conclusions from our journey through Scripture.

First, where does the Bible point us in the practice of prayer? The short answer is "Christ". To explore what that means in practice, we return to the question I posed in Chapter 1: "Does believing come before praying?" What does the Bible say? It speaks of "believing *in*" God and Jesus—that is trusting and committing. Believing *that* (e.g. "God raised Jesus from the dead", Romans 10:9) is important as well. But it's not as important as "believing in", whatever the Church might sometimes seems to suggest. The Apostles' and the Nicene Creeds begin "I/we believe *in* One God . . .". Belief, like prayer, is a living relationship with God and, because of that, with other people.

This brings us to a second feature of praying in the Bible: praying *from the heart*. This is important, as the first commandment, "Love the Lord your God with all your heart" suggests. In the Bible, the "heart" is the centre of a person's being, and particularly their will. (We noted in Chapter 9 the prominence of "heart" language in the Psalms.) The challenge is this: how may we move from praying with the mind to praying from the heart? To put it more concretely, how can we move from saying the Lord's Prayer to living it, from merely reciting "Your kingdom come" to really longing for that kingdom? The Bible invites us, not just to say our prayers, but to immerse ourselves in prayer. How, otherwise, can we pray "continually" (1 Thessalonians 5:17)?

Old and New Testament alike disturb our assumptions about prayer. True prayer doesn't start with us at all. The Bible, especially the Gospels of Matthew and Luke, confronts us with a searching challenge: if we think we're good at praying, we are likely to be deluding ourselves. On the other hand, "outsiders", with questions, doubts and angry protests galore, may seem to be doing anything but pray, when, in fact, these passionate responses to life often are a kind of praying. Beneath all the anger and doubt there is a hunger for the God in whom the person praying in this way finds it so hard to believe.

As for our reading of the Bible, we noted in Chapter 2 examples of how we read into it ideas and themes which aren't there at all. We have "cherry-picked" from Scripture, finding, sometimes, what we have wanted to find. We've made a saint of busy Martha (Luke 10:38–42), and unbelieving Thomas the patron saint of doubters (John 20:24–29). We've forgotten that being justified by faith means being justified *by God*; even faith is God's gift (Ephesians 2:8). We've let the second commandment of loving our neighbour overshadow "the greatest and first" (Matthew 22:38) commandment of loving God. (In our final section we shall return to the utterly central theme of love.)

As for discipleship and prayer in the Bible, we have heard "Ask and you will receive", but not, perhaps, "Wait silently for God" (Psalm 62:1). We talk far more about "following" Jesus, less about "abiding" in Christ. "Following" is the emphasis of the first three Gospels, "abiding" the emphasis of John, especially John 13–17. (Paul, like John, writes of being "in" Christ.) Yet because we find both John and Paul difficult, we neglect and marginalize both—to the great impoverishment of the churches, and of ourselves as individual Christians.

The transformation from being a follower from a distance—a semi-detached disciple—to abiding in Christ is crucial to Christian spirituality and prayer. It is possible—all too easy—to be very committed to our local church and still be a semi-detached disciple. A "god" (i.e. an idol), even if we think it's the Christian God, can have a deadening effect on our life and our beliefs, especially if we take our "god" for granted, never questioning or examining the childhood faith we inherited. The real God, to whom the Bible bears witness, springs surprises, keeps us moving, disturbs the status quo. If reading the Bible leaves us unchanged or the same kind of Christian we've always been, perhaps we haven't begun really to attend to it.

The Bible's teaching also precludes making our prayers a private affair. Relationships with other people matter supremely. A local church, like a friendship, has to be kept in good repair (and I'm not referring here to the roof). Jesus gave us only one prayer: "Our Father ... ". So: no judging, no grudges, no gossip, no enemies ... or, if we have, we pray for them—regularly.

Growing into prayer and reading the Bible well go together, each enriching the other.

We need an *experience* of the Bible as "a source of life, truth and growth", making us want to read it more. But often we do not read the Bible well because we are not sufficiently recollected and still. In the course of our praying, we need to move from the mind to the heart, from using words to being still and silent. This takes time and practice. It's important not to "beat ourselves up" for our wandering thoughts, or be discouraged by them. In this struggle (as it often is), many have found Christian mantras ("rhythm prayers") a great help.[1]

How much of the Bible we read is not the most important issue. *How* we read it is what matters. We are reading it in order to find, or receive again, the love of God. We read as attentively and prayerfully as we can. The discipline known in some Christian traditions as *Lectio Divina*

---

[1] Even though a rhythm prayer such as "Lord Jesus, have mercy" is repeated like a mantra, it differs from most mantras in that, as a prayer, it is directed to God.

(literally, "divine" or "sacred reading") can help. This simple discipline has four stages: our reading leads us to meditate, then to pray, and, finally, to contemplation. This kind of praying, which has silence and listening at its heart, helps us to read the Bible well.[2] We become sensitive to our preconceptions of what is in the Bible, begin to notice what we had missed before, and to discover new truths even in familiar passages.

The Christian world today is realizing more and more that the world needs a Church which is not only compassionate, but contemplative as well. With that in mind, we return to the story of Martha and Mary (Luke 10:38–42). The difference between the two sisters was not a matter of temperament—Martha a do-er, Mary a pray-er. We might prefer to think that, since busyness can be a great distraction from God. The gentle rebuke of Martha by Jesus makes clear that her heart was not in the right place. She was "worried and distracted" and, we might add, harshly critical of her sister. Such criticism is never a good sign (Matthew 7:1 again: "Judge not . . . ").

In the Christian past, the two sisters have been thought to exemplify two vocations: Mary the contemplative vocation of monks and nuns, Martha the everyday life of everyone else. But this traditional view that contemplation is only for the select few is being increasingly questioned today. Karl Rahner, a great Roman Catholic theologian of the twentieth century, foresaw a time when all Christians would be contemplatives. Thomas Merton wrote of contemplation as "the awakening of Christ within us, the establishment of the Kingdom of God in our own soul".[3]

As for contemplative prayer, there is far more in the Bible about a more attentive, quiet way of praying than first appears. The Psalmists, for example, speak of "waiting on" or "waiting for" God:

For God alone my soul waits in silence.

Psalm 62:1,5

---

[2]   For a recent introduction, see Christine Valters Paintner and Lucy Wynkoop OSB, *Lectio Divina: Contemplative Awakening and Awareness* (Mahwah, NJ: Paulist Press, 2008).

[3]   *The Inner Experience: Notes on Contemplation*, ed. William H. Shannon (London: SPCK, 2003), pp. 33–4.

Most of all, the theme of "abiding" in Christ points towards a deeper, more contemplative way of praying. (Hence the choice of verses at the beginning of this chapter.)

But our final word here must be the point where this section began: Christ is the goal, as he is the Way. We begin truly to pray as we open ourselves to the grace and love of God "through Jesus Christ our Lord", and as the Holy Spirit leads us into "abiding in Christ". How will we know? Love, above all, will be the measure. But there will be other, perhaps quiet indications. A great guide on prayer used to say that the more we pray, the better it goes, where "it" applies both to our praying and to life itself: "the real value of prayer can be . . . estimated by its effect on the rest of the day".[4]

Love answering love: Towards contemplation

One more book in the Bible merits a place in this survey of prayer in the Bible. The Song of Songs in the Old Testament "became part of the Bible . . . because readers felt that its depiction of physical human love is so beautiful and deep that it expresses the love between God and humans better than any other human document".[5] Jewish rabbis and Christian saints have treasured it, calling it "the Holy of Holies". Some of its verses express as well as any in the Bible "love answering love":

> My beloved is mine, and I am his . . .
> Set me as a seal upon your heart,
> . . . for love is strong as death . . .
> Many waters cannot quench love . . .
>
> *Song of Songs 2:16; 8:6–7*

---

[4]   *The Spiritual Letters of Dom John Chapman OSB* (London: Sheed and Ward, 1935), p. 291.

[5]   *The Wesley Study Bible* (Nashville, TN: Abingdon Press, 2019), p. 805. For additional guidance on the Song of Songs, see also Graeme Watson, *The Song of Songs: A Contemplative Guide* (London: SPCK, 2014).

Its reception as Scripture confirms the central place of Love not only in the Bible, but in creation and human life.

Except in emergencies, many of us—perhaps most of the human race—tend to hide from God, forget about God, take God for granted, or not believe in God at all. As for being a "sinner", as the Bible seems to insist, that, we think, is surely an overstatement. It's other people who are sinners. (We can always think of someone to look down on.) Thinking of ourselves as sinners may not be a healthy thing to do, anyway, if we suffer from low self-esteem. (Chapter 6, and the section on confession, offers a corrective to much Christian thinking about this.)

So what do we need? The following words, I believe, provide the Bible's answer:

> Most people . . . think because they are sinners, they are not lovable. But what sin really means is that they are not loving. These are two different things. *We are always lovable because God loves us.*[6]

We easily misread or mishear the Bible. Many of us who go to church will have heard often the stories of Jesus' baptism and transfiguration, including God's word to Jesus, "This is my beloved Son" (e.g. Matthew 3:17; 17:5). What we've failed to hear is that those words apply equally to us. Jesus wasn't called God's son because he had earned that accolade, and two verses which refer to Jesus as God's "only begotten" Son (John 1:18; 3:16) mean the true origin of Jesus lay in the mystery of God's own being, not that Jesus can't have brothers and sisters like ourselves.

We need to become better listeners and readers of the Bible. When Paul (and other New Testament writers) called their churches "beloved", they meant *God* loved them, and that's why Paul loved them. Romans 1:7 makes it quite clear: "*God's* beloved"—and that, not because they had now become Christians and therefore qualified for that love. (Remember

---

[6] John J. English SJ, *Spiritual Freedom: From an Experience of the Ignatian Exercise to the Art of Spiritual Guidance* (Chicago: Loyola Press, 1995), pp. 55–6, my italics.

the prodigal son.) All too easily, our hearts and our consciences tell us we must earn or qualify for God's love. But that is not the Bible's message.

Christian faith tells us that Love is where our human story began, and where, by the grace of God, it will end. The longing for God lies deep within us all. That is how we are made. But we are easily distracted and discouraged. Even if we are inescapably busy—I'm thinking especially of parents of young children, full-time carers, and people obliged to work long hours—we can still "cry to the Lord from the depths"—that is, *from the heart.* In such situations, we must draw encouragement from the fact that every word and action spoken or done in love will keep us near the God who is love (1 John 4:8,16). In the words of the old hymn, "we should *never* be discouraged".

Believing in God means, in practice, putting more of ourselves into what we have to do each day. That applies both to our reading of the Bible and our prayers. The will and the intention are what matter most. "Search the Scriptures" was the advice of John Wesley; above all, seek Christ within its pages. In both praying and Bible-reading, seek God. If we seek God with all our heart, we shall surely find him (Deuteronomy 4:29).

Prayer mysteriously simplifies life; it helps us to distinguish the things that really matter from the things that matter less, to see life, other people, and ourselves more clearly—and, sometimes, to see God in people and in situations where we had not seen God before. There is something both profound *and simple* at the heart of what the Bible teaches about prayer. But the truest measure of progress in prayer is Love; there is no other. However slowly and uncertainly, through setbacks and failures, prayer leads us along the way of love. It is "love answering love".

A brief postscript

This book was initially completed during the winter of 2018–19, a time of multiple crises. Since then, much has happened. The Covid pandemic struck almost the whole world, and we are still not entirely free of it. Still more crises and dangers, such as Russia's invasion of Ukraine, have emerged. Ever more urgent UN reports continue to stress how little time we have left to "fix the planet"—that is, to save ourselves from catastrophic, irreversible climate change. My own country, the UK, seems to lurch from one crisis to another.

Against this background, I venture to hope that this book may be a resource for Christian living and resilience "for the living of these days". But as I write, in the autumn of 2022, I hope also that the book will not encourage a Christian pietism which does not seriously engage with the world. (And we Christians can be endlessly self-deluding about this matter.)

To fail to pray is a "failure to find time for reality" (E. Underhill). Real prayer affects the whole of life and embraces the world. Christianity is about our humanness. Whatever it might sometimes look like, the Church is called to be the *human* institution *par excellence.* Christian baptism means joining—fully and whole-heartedly—the human race. To pray is a journey towards becoming the human being God created us to be, and to embrace the world and its people in all their suffering and beauty, strengths and weaknesses.[7] We cannot ring-fence Christian prayer from anything. "The creation waits with eager longing for the revealing of the children of God" (Romans 8:19). The Bible's final prayer (Revelation 22:20) seems a fitting finale: "Amen. Come, Lord Jesus!"

Prayers

Almighty God, help me so to seek you that I may truly find you, and use even my prayers in your grand project to bring healing, life and light to your world.

---

[7]   On these themes see also my *Waking Up to God. Re-discovering Faith in Post-Pandemic Times* (Durham: Sacristy Press, 2022).

Father God,
you have created all things
and through Christ revealed your salvation
in all the world.
Give us a vision of your glory
and by your Holy Spirit fill us with life and love
that we may praise and serve you
through Jesus Christ our Lord,
who is alive and reigns with you,
in the unity of the Holy Spirit,
one God for ever and ever. Amen.
(Collect for Trinity Sunday)

For reflection and discussion

1. How can we nurture an enthusiastic engagement with the Bible?
2. How may we help each other to move from the mind to the heart in our praying?
3. What is God calling us to do this year in the service of a broken world?

Ingram Content Group UK Ltd.
Milton Keynes UK
UKHW021834030523
421181UK00013B/902